We the People...

Teacher's Guide

Level I
Upper Elementary

Center for Civic Education 5146 Douglas Fir Road • Calabasas, CA 91302 • (818) 591-9321

Directed by the
Center for Civic Education
and
Funded by the
U.S. Department of Education by act of Congress
Established 1987 under the
Commission on the Bicentennial of the United States Constitution

Cover: "Jolly Flatboatmen," 1848, George Caleb Bingham
Daniel J. Terra Collection
Terra Museum of American Art, Chicago

Copyright Center for Civic Education 1988
Eighth Printing 1996

ISBN 0-89818-111-9

Acknowledgments

The following staff and consultants have contributed to the development of this text.

Editorial Directors
Charles N. Quigley
Duane E. Smith
Jane G. Sure

General Editor
Judith A. Matz

Production Directors
Evelyn C. Davis
Kerin Martin
Patricia Mathwig
Theresa Richard

Staff Associates
Arlene Chatman
Michael Leong
Alita Letwin
Louis E. Rosen
Howard Safier

Consulting Associates
Gloria Eastman
Leslie Hendrikson
Barbara Miller
Eugenia Moore
David Morgan
Laurel Singleton
John Zola

Art Director and Illustrator
Richard Stein

Typesetters
Roslyn Danberg
Jan Ruyle

Production Assistant
Lise Borja

The Center is also grateful for the many helpful comments and suggestions that have been received from the following persons who have reviewed the manuscript in its various developmental stages. The Center has attempted to be responsive to all of the many valuable suggestions for improvement in the text. However, the final product is the responsibility of the Center and does not necessarily reflect the views of those who have contributed their thoughts and ideas.

A. L. Block
Director of Instruction
Franklin School District
Franklin, Wisconsin

Margaret Branson
Administrator
Division of Instructional Services
Kern County Public Schools
Kern Country, California

Gary Bryner
Professor
Department of Political Science
Brigham Young University
Provo, Utah

Libby Cupp
Coordinator
Consumer Affairs
Apollo Career Center
Lima, Ohio

Lorenca Rosal Douglas
Executive Director
New Hampshire Law Related
Education
Concord, New Hampshire

Tami Dowler
Area Director for UniServ
Kentucky Education
Association
Frankfort, Kentucky

Michael Fischer
Associate
Bureau of Social Studies
New York State Education
Department
Albany, New York

James R. Giese
Executive Director
Social Science Education
Consortium, Inc.
Boulder, Colorado

Jeanne Kress
Teacher
Country Dale Elementary School
Franklin, Wisconsin

Joan Parrish
Demonstration Teacher
Corinne A. Seeds University
Elementary School
Westwood, California

Dorothy Skeel
Director
Peabody Center for Economic
and Social Studies
George Peabody College of
Vanderbilt University
Nashville, Tennessee

Connie Yeaton
Coordinator
Indiana State Law Related
Education Project of the
Indiana Bar Association
Columbus, Ohio

Warren E. Burger, Chairman

Commission on the Bicentennial of the United States Constitution

Chief Justice of the United States, 1969-1986

The years 1987 to 1991 marked the 200th anniversary of the writing, ratification, and implementation of the basic documents of American democracy, the Constitution and the Bill of Rights. Our Constitution has stood the tests and stresses of time, wars and change. Although it was not perfect, as Benjamin Franklin and many others recognized, it has lasted because it was carefully crafted by men who understood the importance of a system of government sufficiently strong to meet the challenges of the day, yet sufficiently flexible to accommodate and adapt to new political, economic, and social conditions.

Many Americans have but a slight understanding of the Constitution, the Bill of Rights, and the later amendments to which we pledge our allegiance. The lessons in this book are designed to give you, the next generation of American citizens, an understanding of the background, creation, and subsequent history of the unique system of government brought into being by our Constitution. At the same time, it will help you understand the principles and ideals that underlie and give meaning to the Constitution, a system of government by those governed.

Table of Contents

Introduction   1

Unit One   What were the Founders' basic ideas about government?   3

Lesson 1.   What was America like in the 1770s?   5

Lesson 2.   Why did the Founders think we needed a government?   8

Lesson 3.   What is a republican government?   11

Lesson 4.   What is a constitutional government?   13

Lesson 5.   How did the Founders use their ideas in the Declaration   16
             of Independence?

Lesson 6.   What was our first national government like?   20

Unit Two   How was our Constitution written?   24

Lesson 7.   How did the Philadelphia Convention begin?   25

Lesson 8.   How many representatives should each state have in Congress?   28

Lesson 9.   How should the problem of slavery be handled?   32

Lesson 10.   What basic ideas are in the Preamble to the Constitution?   35

Unit Three   How did the Framers organize our government?   37

Lesson 11.   How did the Framers limit the powers of our government?   38

Lesson 12.   What is the legislative branch?   40

Lesson 13.   What is the executive branch?   44

Lesson 14.   What is the judicial branch?   48

Lesson 15.   What is a federal government?   50

Unit Four   **How does the Constitution protect your basic rights?**   52

   Lesson 16.   How does the Constitution protect your freedom of expression?   53

   Lesson 17.   How does the Constitution protect your freedom of religion?   56

   Lesson 18.   How does the Constitution protect your right to be treated   59
                 equally by the government?

   Lesson 19.   How does the Constitution protect your right to be treated   61
                 fairly by the government?

   Lesson 20.   How does the Constitution protect your right to vote?   64

Unit Five   **What are the responsibilities of citizens?**   69

   Lesson 21.   What responsibilities accompany our rights?   70

   Lesson 22.   How can we promote the common welfare?   72

Reference Section

   Declaration of Independence   77

   Constitution of the United States   81

   Biographies of Important Framers   94

   Glossary   98

   Suggested Reading   102

Introduction

We the People ... introduces elementary students to the study of constitutional government in the United States. It is not a conventional history text focusing on people and events. This book is a history of ideas. It is designed to help elementary students understand the most important ideas of our constitutional system and how they were developed. Its intent is to provide students with a knowledge of how the Constitution came into existence, why it took the form it did, and how it has functioned for the past two hundred years. By gaining such an understanding, students will be preparing themselves for the responsibilities of citizenship.

Teaching Methods

Level I of *We the People* ... is designed to be used in the upper elementary grades. The program employs a conceptually oriented approach that stresses the development of analytic and evaluative skills. Because many of the concepts introduced in the program may be unfamiliar to students, the methodology draws heavily on strategies that research and field testing have shown to be successful in developing conceptual understanding. Students will learn how to apply their understanding and knowledge to a wide variety of political questions and issues. They will develop the skills to relate their everyday experiences to basic issues of constitutional government and civic responsibility.

Teaching strategies are varied, including directed discussions, simulations, debates, role playing, timeline construction, and small-group problem solving. The program allows for and depends upon a wide use of interdisciplinary skills. Art, spelling, vocabulary, mathematics, writing, research, and social studies skills are all incorporated in the structure of these lessons.

Lesson Format

This teacher's guide is designed to complement and extend the student text. Each student lesson begins with the "Purpose of Lesson"—a brief narrative passage designed to stimulate student interest and to guide the reading of the text.

The narrative for each lesson is divided into small segments to make it manageable for students. Strategies for presenting and discussing these materials are given in the TEACHING PROCEDURES segment of the lesson plans. Skill-building activities are presented within the student text. In some lessons, the text introduces the key concepts, which are then reinforced through an activity. In other lessons, the activity introduces the concepts and is followed by an explanation and discussion of the concepts.

The lessons include illustrations designed to complement and enhance comprehension of the narrative material. Each illustration is accompanied by a question and requires students to interpret information, apply facts, theorize, think creatively, use deductive reasoning, and employ decision-making skills. The illustrations lend themselves to small group or interactive teaching strategies.

New vocabulary terms are highlighted in the student text and defined either within the narrative itself or in the outside column next to the text. Definitions explain the usage of the word in its specific textual context. All terms are also defined in the glossary at the end of the student text.

At the end of the review section of each lesson, students are asked to explain the meaning of the new terms used in that lesson. A variety of vocabulary-building activities can be employed to reinforce understanding of the new terms. Students can be asked to create their own dictionaries which they may also wish to illustrate. They may be asked to write sentences that use each of the terms. A vocabulary test or a writing assignment could be used at the end of the unit as a check for understanding. Another option would be a class spelling bee which required students to use the term correctly in a sentence as well as spell it.

Each lesson in the student text ends with a list of questions entitled "Reviewing and using the lesson," which can be used as a basis for concluding the class discussions. Questions may also be assigned for either individual or small-group homework assignments.

Additional and alternative activities to reinforce, extend, and enrich the concepts of the lesson are included in the OPTIONAL ACTIVITIES portion of the lesson plan. These should be considered since many stimulating and exciting strategies are located in this part of the lesson plan.

Unit Format

In the Teacher's Guide, the unit overview provides a brief introduction to the forthcoming group of lessons and their objectives. In many of the units, an optional unit project is also suggested. These special projects are varied—some are individual activities and some meant for small-group work—designed to complement the class projects which students will be working on throughout their course of study.

Introducing the Book

Inform the students that they are about to begin a study of the Constitution of the United States. Explain that the text will provide them with an understanding of how the Constitution came into existence, why it took the form it did, and how it has worked for the past two hundred years.

Have students locate the Table of Contents and read aloud the titles to each of the units. Point out that each unit title and each lesson title asks a question. Tell students that they will learn the answers to these questions as they study each lesson. Ask students to locate the Reference Section and discuss with them the contents of this section and how it can be used.

Next have the students turn to the Introduction to the text. Read the Introduction with the students and have them answer the two questions in "Reviewing important ideas."

Class Projects

Go over that portion of the Introduction that deals with the class project—a bulletin board display, including a timeline and an illustrated map of the original thirteen colonies.

- The bulletin board display can include articles, pictures, stories, poems, art work, and newspaper headlines which illustrate the key ideas and events in each lesson. In Units Three, Four, and Five, the display could demonstrate the relevance of the lessons to current political activities.

- The bulletin board display can include a timeline which will show the events that are being studied. Students may wish to add additional dates and events not mentioned in the text. The timeline might be constructed above the bulletin board and chalkboard. Another method of displaying a timeline would be to "hang" the dates to a rope or on a clothesline. Students might want to post and illustrate the dates.

- The class may also illustrate an outline map of the original thirteen states. On this map, students can place pictures of important events, people, or facts about the states they are studying. One method to do such a map would be to divide the class into 13 groups. Each group would be responsible for one of the 13 states. Each group would then explain to the class their reasons for selecting the facts, persons, or events they chose to illustrate.

2

Unit One

What were the Founders' basic ideas about government?

UNIT OVERVIEW

This unit contains six lessons that help students understand who the Founders were and what ideas and experiences shaped their thinking about government. Students begin their study by learning what life was like in America in the 1770s. The next three lessons are devoted to a consideration of the Founders' ideas about government.

In Lesson 2, students are introduced to the Founders' beliefs about natural rights and the purpose of government. They consider questions such as: What might happen if there were no government? What should governments do? Where do governments get their right to govern? Lesson 3 presents another important idea that influenced the Framers—republicanism—and focuses on why they were convinced that a republic was the best kind of government for Americans. In the fourth lesson, students are introduced to the idea of constitutionalism and asked to consider the question, "Why is it important to limit the powers of the government?"

With this background, students study the events that led to the American Revolution and analyze the Declaration of Independence. Unit One concludes with an examination of our first national constitution, the Articles of Confederation, and prepares students to study the Philadelphia Convention in the following unit.

UNIT OBJECTIVES

At the conclusion of this unit:

1. Students should be able to describe the characteristics of life in the United States during the 1770s.

2. Students should be able to explain what the Founders meant by natural rights and what they considered to be the purpose of government.

3. Students should be able to explain the characteristics of republican government and to discuss the role of civic virtue.

4. Students should be able to distinguish between constitutional governments and dictatorial governments.

5. Students should be able to explain basic ideas in the Declaration of Independence.

6. Students should be able to describe the Articles of Confederation, discuss achievements under the Articles, explain the weaknesses of the Articles, and describe the concerns that led to the Philadelphia Convention.

UNIT INTRODUCTION

Have students turn to the Introduction to Unit One: "What were the Founders' basic ideas about government?" Read the text with the class, focusing on the topics that will be covered in the unit.

UNIT PROJECT (optional)

In addition to the three class projects listed on page 2 of the Student Book, you may wish to have students develop the following quilt project. Since most early American farm women could quilt, have students create a paper quilt (using crayons or markers) in which each square represents the special characteristics of a particular state. The class could be divided into thirteen small groups, with each group assigned responsibility for researching life in one state and illustrating what they learned in a quilt square(s). For example, squares could depict Founders from that state, important contributions to the American Revolution from that state, or typical scenes from that state during the 1770s.

Lesson 1

What was America like in the 1770s?

LESSON OVERVIEW

This lesson is designed to help students place the events at the Philadelphia Convention in a historical and social context. It provides students with a general description of life in the American colonies in the 1770s. Students consider the geography of the colonies and the diversity of the people. They examine the different life styles in different regions of the country and look at the opportunities available to most colonists. The lesson concludes with a discussion of how Britain ruled the American colonies and the importance of the Founders.

LESSON OBJECTIVES

At the conclusion of this lesson:

1. Students should be able to describe who the American colonists were and how they lived.

2. Students should be able to describe the opportunities available to most Americans and the limitations on these opportunities.

3. Students should be able to describe the effect of Great Britain's early rule of the colonies and the growth of self-government in America.

5. Students should be able to explain what is meant by the term, "Founders," and why the Founders were important.

MATERIALS NEEDED

Student text

TEACHING PROCEDURES

A. Introductory Activity:
Our connection to Great Britain

Have students read the "Purpose of Lesson," "Our country first belonged to Great Britain," and "Turn back the clock." Have students use a map of the world to locate Europe, Great Britain, and North America. Now locate the United States and point out that the American colonies were over two thousand miles away across the Atlantic Ocean.

Ask the students to think about these questions:

- What would it be like to live in a colony of another country?

- What would it be like to live over two thousand miles away from the mother country?

- Would you want to live under the rule of a monarch? Why or why not?

- Would you want to live in a time of revolutionary change such as the 1770s?

B. Reading and Discussion:
Understanding America's geography 200 years ago

Have students read the section "What was America like 200 years ago?" Discuss with students the possible influence of sparse population and vast amounts of land on a people's attitudes toward the future. Possible discussion questions could be:

- If land is cheap and there is plenty of water, how might this affect the way you farm? If there are abundant natural resources, how might this affect the cutting of trees for lumber or firewood?

- If the means of transportation are slow and primitive, how might this affect your life? What would be the effect of long distances between you and your neighbors?

C. Reading and Discussion:
Understanding diversity in early America

Have students read the section "Who were the Americans?" Discuss the diverse groups that lived in the colonies at that time and the similarities and differences that existed among them.

D. Reading and Discussion:
Understanding how Americans lived in the 1770s

Divide the class into groups of three to five students. Have students read the section "How did Americans live?" and discuss how their lives today are different from those of Americans of the 1770s. Ask students to explain why they would or would not like to have lived in America during that time.

As an optional activity, have students look at the illustrations and question on page 9 of the text. Divide students into several groups to prepare for a role play of a dinner conversation between a Northern farm family and a Southern slave-holding family. Half of the groups will play the role of the Southern family and the other half will play the Northern family. Each group can choose the colony its members are residing in. Groups are to write a script for the dinner table conversation. One Southern family and one Northern family should be brought together to stage their conversation for the rest of the class. Record the differences between their lives on the chalkboard or chart paper.

E. Reading and Discussion:
Examining opportunities in early America

Have students read "Opportunities in America." Discuss the advantages of life in America at that time, and ask which groups did not share these advantages. You might wish to include questions 3 and 5 from "Reviewing and using the lesson" in your class discussion.

F. Reading and Discussion:
The role of Great Britain in governing colonial America

Have students read "Who governed the colonies?" and "Who were the Founders?" Ask them to consider the effects of British policy, which essentially ignored the colonies for most of this period. As a preparation for later lessons, students could think about what might happen if Britain decided to tighten its control over the colonies.

The students are introduced in this lesson to the term "Founders." They might discuss Founders they are familiar with, such as George Washington. You might ask them why they think most of the Founders were men.

G. Concluding Activity

Conclude the lesson by discussing the questions in "Reviewing and using the lesson." At this time, students can be introduced to the unit projects and organized into groups to work on these projects. A vocabulary-building activity for this text may also be introduced at this time. Students should begin by including the new terms they have learned in this lesson.

OPTIONAL ACTIVITIES

For Reinforcement, Extended Learning, and Enrichment

1. Have students make detailed maps of America in the 1770s, showing population centers and transportation routes as well as colonial boundaries.

2. What was life like for a child in the 1770s? Have students write what their life would be like if they lived in America in the 1770s.

3. Have selected groups of students research the "lifestyle" of an ethnic group during this early American period.

4. Have students research and report on the status of colonial women. Political and legal rights, educational opportunities, and household duties should be covered.

5. The style of clothing worn during the colonial period had its origins in the fashions of the nobility and aristocracy. However, many Americans were not at all interested in this fashion. Have students read *Why Don't You Get a Horse, Sam Adams?* by Jean Fritz, and write a book report on the view of this famous American.

Lesson 2

Why did the Founders think we needed a government?

LESSON OVERVIEW

This lesson introduces the basic concepts of the natural rights philosophy. Although they may not be familiar with the terms used by natural rights philosophers to describe these ideas, students will be familiar with the ideas as they are closely related to their experiences.

The lesson opens by involving the students in a problem-solving activity, asking them to identify what they think are their basic rights. They learn that the Founders called these rights our natural rights and were concerned with how to protect them. Students then engage in a second problem-solving activity, exploring what life would be like without any rules or laws. Students learn that people consent to form a government in order to protect their rights.

Since many of the ideas in the remaining lessons are based on the concepts presented in Lesson 2, teachers may want to devote extra time to ensuring that students understand these ideas.

LESSON OBJECTIVES

At the conclusion of this lesson:

1. Students should be able to explain the Founders' beliefs about natural rights.

2. Students should be able to explain what problems might occur in a world without rules or laws and compare their ideas with those of the Founders.

3. Students should be able to explain the purpose of government discussed in this lesson.

MATERIALS NEEDED

1. Student text

2. Handout 2-1 (optional)

TEACHING PROCEDURES

A. Introduction and Problem Solving:
Defining "rights"

Have the students read the "Purpose of Lesson." Then organize the class into groups of 3-5 students and read the problem-solving activity aloud, allowing time for questions. Ask each group to develop answers to the three questions in the activity and to write its answers on chart paper. Call on a member of each group to report its responses to the rest of the class and to post their chart paper on the wall. Compare the lists of the various groups, asking students to find and discuss the:

- similarities between the different groups' lists of rights;

- differences between the different groups' lists of rights.

B. Reading and Discussion:
Defining natural rights

Have the section "What were the Founders' beliefs about rights?" read orally. Discuss the terms introduced in this section, such as "life," "liberty," "property," and "natural rights," to be sure the students understand and can explain their meaning. Then compare these "natural rights" to those students had identified in the problem-solving activity. Discuss the similarities and differences between the beliefs of the Founders and their own. You may wish to ask students to hypothesize as to why these similarities and differences exist.

C. Problem Solving:
Examining life without rules, laws, or government

Ask students to look at the illustration on page 17 of the student text, identify what is taking place, and answer the accompanying question "How can we protect our rights?" Then ask them to read and discuss the major ideas in the section "Why do we need to protect our rights?"

Read through the problem-solving activity with the class and then organize the class into groups of 3-5 students. Each group is to develop answers to the questions, with each student writing down the group's responses. (In this way every member of the group is responsible for focusing on the discussion and being prepared to report back to the class.)

You may wish to have students in each group share experiences they have had in which a problem arose because there were no rules, laws, or people to enforce them. Have each group share their responses with the class.

D. Reading and Discussion:
Comparing the students' ideas with those of the Founders

Have students read the remainder of the lesson and compare their lists of problems with those of the Founders. Be sure students understand the concept of "consent" contained in the final selection.

E. Concluding Activity

Conclude the lesson with a discussion of the questions in "Reviewing and using the lesson." If classroom time is not available, question 4 might be assigned as homework. Students should also review the new terms in this lesson and add them to their vocabulary-building activity. Time might also be given for students to work on their unit projects.

OPTIONAL ACTIVITIES

For Reinforcement, Extended Learning, and Enrichment

1. Have students complete Handout 2-1, which asks them to come up with some solutions to the problems of a "life without rules." Discuss the solutions with the entire class.

2. Suggest the book *Paradise Island* by W. Harmon Wilson and Roman F. Warmke and ask students to write a book report on the way in which the residents of the island reorganized their government.

3. Have students keep a list of times they see people's rights violated during a one-week period. They could include situations seen at school, on television, in newspapers, or in the community. Ask them to identify the right involved and explain why they believe that right was violated.

Handout 2-1

Solving the problems in a state of nature

Scene 1. This classroom has no rules. There is no one in authority—no one with the right to tell others what to do.

- What problems do you see?
- What rights are being taken away?

_____

_____

_____

_____

_____

Scene 2. This picture shows how one person with authority tried to solve some of the problems you identified.

- List some of the solutions you see in the picture.
- What have the students gained?
- What have the students lost?

_____

_____

_____

_____

_____

_____

What is a republican government?

LESSON OVERVIEW

Many of the ideas that influenced the Founders originated in the government of the Roman Republic. This lesson provides an opportunity for students to explore the meaning of republicanism, common welfare, and civic virtue as they were said to have been practiced in ancient Rome, and to consider how these ideas influenced the thinking and behavior of the Founders.

The lesson opens with a brief description of republican government in Rome and a discussion of what the Founders thought were the principal characteristics and advantages of republican government. Students engage in a problem-solving activity examining some of the considerations involved in determining the common welfare. Students then read about the Founders' belief in the importance of civic virtue in creating a republican government.

LESSON OBJECTIVES

At the conclusion of this lesson:

1. Students should be able to explain why the Founders thought republican government was the best type of government.

2. Students should be able to discuss the importance of the concepts of the common welfare and civic virtue in a republican government.

MATERIALS NEEDED

Student text

TEACHING PROCEDURES

A. Reading and Discussion:
Understanding the influence of the Roman Republic

Have students read the "Purpose of Lesson," "The Founders studied history" and "What is a republican government?" Make sure that students understand the three elements of a republic that the Founders believed were important.

B. Reading and Discussion:
Understanding the advantages of republican government

Have students read the next two sections, "What are the advantages of republican government?" and "What is the common welfare?" Review with the students what the Founders believed were the advantages of a republican form of government.

Write the words "common welfare" on the board and discuss the meaning of each word and the entire phrase.

Ask students to examine the picture on page 23 of the student text and answer the question "Is this government serving the common welfare?" Explain that deciding what is the common welfare and who should have the power to make that decision is not always easy. The next problem-solving activity should help them understand this difficulty.

C. Problem Solving:
Determining the common welfare

Read the problem-solving activity "Your interests and the common welfare" with the class. Then divide the class into groups of 3-5 students. Ask each group to develop responses to the four situations given. You may wish to have one student act as chairperson of the group and assign each of the other students one of the situations listed. The chairperson should write down and report the group's response to the class.

In addition, you may wish to assign each group one of the situations and have them create a skit to depict their responses. Culminate the activity by having the groups share their opinions and their skits.

D. Reading and Discussion:
Understanding the importance of civic virtue

Have the students read the section "What is civic virtue?" Discuss the meaning and importance of civic virtue. Ask students why they think civic virtue is necessary in a republican form of government. You might ask students to provide examples of civic virtue from their own lives.

E. Concluding Activity

Conclude the lesson by discussing the questions contained in "Reviewing and using the lesson." Groups should continue work on their unit projects and their vocabulary-building activity.

OPTIONAL ACTIVITIES

For Reinforcement, Extended Learning, and Enrichment

1. Have students analyze nursery rhymes, fairy tales, and Aesops Fables to determine if they promote civic virtue.

2. Ask students to write a report on a television show which encourages young people to develop civic virtue.

3. Invite a representative of local, state, or national government to speak to the class. Ask the person to provide examples of government actions that serve the common welfare.

What is a constitutional government?

LESSON OVERVIEW

This lesson introduces students to key concepts in understanding the Founders' ideas about government. Students learn the meaning of "constitution" and what distinguishes a constitution from other rules and laws. They then examine the essential characteristics that differentiate constitutional government from dictatorial government. They learn that in a constitutional government the powers of the person or group running the government are limited by a constitution that must be obeyed. Through the use of a problem-solving activity involving a selection from *Two Years Before the Mast*, students learn of the dangers of a government with unlimited power.

LESSON OBJECTIVES

At the conclusion of this lesson:

1. Students should be able to define "constitution" and "constitutional government."

2. Students should be able to explain the difference between a constitutional government and a dictatorial government.

3. Students should be able to explain the importance of limiting the powers of government.

MATERIALS NEEDED

Student text

TEACHING PROCEDURES

A. Introductory Activity:
Identifying different kinds of laws

Write the following headings on the chalkboard:

Rules and Laws that:

Tell how government is
to be run

Do not tell how government
is to be run

Read the "Purpose of Lesson" with the class. Organize the class into groups of 3-5 students and have them read the instructions given in the problem-solving activity. Ask each group to make a chart on a piece of paper that looks like the one on the chalkboard and to work together to fill it out. When each group is finished, call on students to help you fill out the chart on the board, explaining how and why they classified each rule or law.

B. Reading and Discussion:
What is a constitution?

Have the students read the first two paragraphs of the section on "What is a constitution?" and ask them to define what a constitution is. Then have them read the remainder of the section. Outline with them the questions that a constitution should answer. Help students understand that these are questions that all constitutions answer. Hence, every nation has a constitution, whether the government is fair or unfair.

C. Reading and Discussion:
Identifying a constitutional government

Have students read "What is a constitutional government?" Discuss the fact that a constitutional government is one in which there are limits on the powers of the people running the government. Furthermore, in a constitutional government, there must be ways to ensure that these limits are obeyed.

Ask students to look at the illustration on page 29 and answer the accompanying question. Explain that trial by jury is one way in which a constitutional government can limit power. Tell students that as they study more about the U.S. Constitution, they will learn other ways that the power of government is limited.

D. Reading and Discussion:
Identifying a dictatorial government

Have students read "What is a dictatorial government?" Ask them to describe the differences between constitutional and dictatorial governments. Discuss how a country with a constitution still might not have a constitutional government. Ask students to look at the illustration on page 30 and discuss with them the question, "What can happen when a ruler has unlimited power?"

E. Problem Solving:
Understanding the need to limit power

Read with the class "Why is it important to limit a government's powers?" Explain to students that after they read the story, "Life on a sailing ship," they will answer the questions at the end.

This exercise may be completed either as an individual or group activity. If you wish to utilize small groups, divide the class into groups of 3-5 students. Assign one student in each group the task of writing down and reporting the group's responses to the class. Lead a class discussion of the questions.

Before discussing the fifth question (What laws would you suggest should be made to protect the rights of the sailors?), you may wish to have students role play a board of inquiry as described in number 3 of "Reviewing and using the lesson." One person from each group could be assigned to the inquiry board, sharing his or her group's responses for suggested new policies.

F. Concluding Activity

Conclude the lesson by leading a discussion of the questions contained in "Reviewing and using the lesson." Allow time for students to work on the unit project. Students should include the new terms in this lesson in their vocabulary-building activity.

OPTIONAL ACTIVITIES

For Reinforcement, Extended Learning, and Enrichment

1. Read the Dr. Seuss book, *Yertle the Turtle* to the class. Then ask students to hypothesize what type of government is represented in the story. Ask what problems and solutions come out of the story.

2. Again using the story *Yertle the Turtle,* have students work together to reorganize Yertle's government so that he could no longer abuse his power. How would the new government work?

3. As a research project, ask students to find an example of a country with an unwritten constitution. (examples: Great Britain, Israel). Ask them to describe what they think would be the advantages and disadvantages of having an unwritten constitution.

How did the Founders use their ideas in the Declaration of Independence?

LESSON OVERVIEW

This lesson deals with the events that led to the American Revolution and introduces students to the Declaration of Independence. Students study the main ideals, arguments, and complaints of the Declaration. They read a key section of the document, explained in language they can understand, and then have an opportunity to rewrite that section in their own words. The lesson concludes with a problem-solving activity that reinforces some of the key concepts in the lesson by allowing students to role play the position of either the Patriots or the Loyalists.

LESSON OBJECTIVES

At the conclusion of this lesson:

1. Students should be able to explain why the colonists revolted against British rule.

2. Students should be able to explain the purposes of the Declaration of Independence.

3. Students should be able to explain the ideals, complaints, and arguments of the Declaration.

MATERIALS NEEDED

1. Student text

2. Handout 5-1 (optional)

TEACHING PROCEDURES

A. Introductory Activity:
Examining the desire for independence

Have students read the "Purpose of Lesson." Ask students to look at the series of three pictures on pages 35 and 36 showing the changing relationship between the colonists and Great Britain. Discuss with the class what they think is happening in these pictures. With this as a background, have students read "Why did the Founders want independence?" In reviewing the background of the American Revolution, emphasize the British position as well as that of the colonists. Point out to the students that many colonists supported the British position and these people became known as Loyalists during the Revolution.

B. Reading and Discussion:
Understanding the need for the Declaration

Have students read "Why was the Declaration of Independence written?" You might wish to discuss Thomas Jefferson with the students. Remind them that, although he was a Founder and later became President, Jefferson was not one of the Framers because he was in France at the time of the Philadelphia Convention. Point out to the students that in 1776 Jefferson was a young man and not considered a good public speaker but his talents as a writer and working with people in small groups were well respected. Discuss with the class the power of ideas and the importance of writing them down for others to read.

C. Reading and Discussion:
Understanding the components of the Declaration

Read aloud with the class the section, "What does the Declaration of Independence say?" Tell students they will be working in groups of six to study the main components of the Declaration. In each group, students will have the following assignments:

- Students 1 and 2 will read and explain the "Ideals of the Declaration" to the rest of the group members.

- Students 3 and 4 will be responsible for "Complaints of the Declaration," and will explain the main ideas in this section.

- Students 5 and 6 will read and explain the main points of the "Arguments of the Declaration."

After each pair of students has explained its assigned section to the rest of the group, review with the entire class the material they have just studied. Be sure that all students understand the concepts presented in these sections.

Review with students the ideas about natural rights and government they have studied and be certain they are able to explain how the Founders used these ideas in the Declaration. At this point, have students read the section of the Declaration contained in question six of "Reviewing and using the lesson." After discussing the ideas contained in this section, students may be asked to complete Handout 5-1 for reinforcement.

D. Problem Solving:
Determining which side to support

Read aloud with the class the directions for the problem-solving activity, "Which side would you support?" Discuss the difficulty many colonists felt in deciding whether or not to support the Revolution. Explain that most colonists considered themselves loyal subjects of Great Britain. When the time came, after the Declaration of Independence, to choose sides, many of these colonists continued to remain loyal to King George III. The Loyalists felt that Britain had supported the colonies and provided for their defense. For this reason, as well as a sense of tradition and loyalty to the Mother Country, intensified frequently by family or official connections, many Americans were unwilling to break their ties with Britain. On the other hand, the Patriots were those who severed their ties with Britain and followed the cause of independence.

After clarifying the position of both sides with the students, divide the class into small groups and have them complete the problem-solving activity. Each group should then share its picture or letter with the rest of the class. The class should decide, according to the arguments presented by the groups, which side they would support, Patriot or Loyalist.

E. Concluding Activity

Conclude the lesson by leading a discussion of the remaining questions contained in "Reviewing and using the lesson." Students should add the new terms in the lesson to their vocabulary-building activity. Allow time for students to work on their projects.

OPTIONAL ACTIVITIES

For Reinforcement, Extended Learning, and Enrichment

1. Have students read (or read to the class) one of the following books by Jean Fritz: *Can't You Make Them Behave, King George?* or *Would You Please Sign Here, John Hancock?*

2. Have students role play possible reactions of King George III to the Declaration of Independence.

3. Distribute copies of Handout 5-1 or write the contents of the Handout on the chalkboard. Have students reread the section of the Declaration on page 41 of the student text and ask them to complete the Handout.

4. Have students present brief reports on the five members of the committee that wrote the Declaration of Independence—Thomas Jefferson, Benjamin Franklin, John Adams, Roger Sherman, and Robert Livingston.

Analyzing the Declaration of Independence

The Declaration of Independence contains many of the Founders' beliefs about government. Reread the passage from the Declaration in your text. Try to find words or phrases that show the beliefs listed in the chart below. Complete the chart by writing in the words from the Declaration.

Beliefs	Words from Declaration that show beliefs
Natural Rights	
Source of natural rights	
Purpose of government	
Consent of the governed	
Right of people to change their government	

What was our first national government like?

LESSON OVERVIEW

This lesson looks at how the Founders created our first national government. Students learn that most of the Founders feared a strong national government. As a result, the government they established under the Articles of Confederation had very limited powers. Students will explore the achievements and problems of the national government under the Articles. They will see how the weaknesses of that government led many people to urge that the Articles of Confederation be strengthened. Lesson 6 gives students the background to understand the Philadelphia Convention of 1787.

LESSON OBJECTIVES

At the conclusion of this lesson:

1. Students should be able to explain some of the fears that shaped our first national government.

2. Students should be able to describe some of the achievements of the government under America's first constitution, the Articles of Confederation.

3. Students should be able to describe some of the problems of the United States under the Articles of Confederation.

MATERIALS NEEDED

1. Student text

2. Handout 6-1 (optional)

TEACHING PROCEDURES

A. Introductory Activity:
Creating a new government

Read the "Purpose of Lesson" with the class. Then review with the students the reasons for the American Revolution and ask them to make a list of fears the Founders might have had about a national government. Read with the class, "What kind of government should we create?" and compare the fears identified in the text with those on the list created by the students.

Review with students the main features of the new government created under the Articles of Confederation.

B. Reading and Discussion:
Reviewing the achievements under the Articles

Have students read "Achievements under the Articles of Confederation." Emphasize that the national government was responsible for a number of important accomplishments during this time. You may wish to divide the class into four groups and assign each group to report on one of the achievements listed. Students could do additional research as needed.

C. Reading and Discussion:
Examining the problems under the Articles

Have students read "Problems under the Articles of Confederation." Ask them to look at the illustration on page 46. What happened when Congress was too weak to control the states? Have students discuss what they think would happen if each state only thought about its own interests.

Have students read "Shays' Rebellion" and ask them why they think property owners were so frightened by what happened in Massachusetts. You should remind students that the Founders thought the purpose of government is to protect people's rights, including the right to property.

D. Reading and Discussion:
Understanding the call for the Philadelphia Convention

Have students read "How should we improve our national government?" Emphasize that the call for the Philadelphia Convention was for delegates to revise the Articles of Confederation. However, the delegates decided to ignore their instructions and write a new constitution. Students should have, at this point, an understanding of both the Founders' ideas about government and the events that led to the Philadelphia Convention.

E. Concluding Activity

Conclude the lesson by leading a discussion of the questions contained in "Reviewing and using the lesson," emphasizing question number 2. Since this is the final lesson of the unit, students should present their unit projects to the rest of the class.

OPTIONAL ACTIVITIES

For Reinforcement, Extended Learning, or Enrichment

1. Have students participate in a "Your State and Others" role play to learn more about what the United States was like under the Articles of Confederation. See Handout 6-1 for more details.

2. Have students write stories in which they describe what the United States would be like today if the Articles of Confederation had been kept as the Constitution.

3. Individual students might research Shays' Rebellion and then, returning to their time machines, role play a "TV Press Conference," interviewing Daniel Shays and other rebels on why they revolted, the governor on why he called out the militia, and citizens both who supported and opposed the action of Shays.

INSTRUCTIONS FOR HANDOUT 6-1

STEPS

1. Divide the class into small groups of two or three students, and explain that each group is responsible for making important decisions about a new state that has just won its independence. Give each group a copy of Handout 6-1.

2. Have each group report how it handled its tasks. List the problems that might arise between the different states.

3. Ask students to create a system to solve these problems. List solutions on the board. (Someone is likely to mention national government as a possibility.)

DISCUSSION

Debrief the role play by discussing the following questions:

1. How did you feel when other states did not cooperate with your state?

2. What are some of the problems that arise when one state makes laws without referring to the needs of other states?

3. How will these problems influence business and trade?

4. Would you like to live under such a system? Why or why not?

Handout 6-1

Your state and others

BACKGROUND

You are the residents of a former colony that has just gained its independence and become a new state. You must quickly make many important decisions and complete many tasks for your new state. One of the most important of these is the relationship of your state with other states. Work with your fellow "Founders" and complete the following tasks.

TASKS

1. Make up a name for your state (not one of the original 13).

2. Decide what will be your unit of money. Design a unit of money for your state. Will you accept the money of other states?

3. Decide if you will allow people from other states to trade in your state. If so, will you charge a tariff (a fee a state charges on items from other states)? If so, how much will it be?

4. Decide if you will allow people from other states to move to your state.

5. Decide if you will allow other states to use your rivers, ports, and roads. Will you charge them to do so?

6. Decide if you will accept the laws of other states. Will you recognize a marriage made in another state?

7. Decide if you will allow slavery within your state. If not, will you return escaped slaves from another state?

Unit Two

How was our Constitution written?

UNIT OVERVIEW

This unit of four lessons describes the delegates to the Philadelphia Convention and discusses how the convention was organized. Students explore two of the major conflicts facing the Framers: representation in Congress and slavery. Students learn how the Framers resolved these conflicts through compromise. The final lesson analyzes the basic ideas in the Preamble to the Constitution.

UNIT OBJECTIVES

At the conclusion of this unit:

1. Students should be able to identify the Framers and describe some of the important delegates at the Philadelphia Convention. They should also be able to explain how the convention was organized.

2. Students should be able to describe the conflicts at the convention over slavery and representation. They should be able to explain how the Framers settled these conflicts.

3. Students should be able to explain the basic ideas in the Preamble to the Constitution.

UNIT INTRODUCTION

Tell students they are going to be learning about the Philadelphia Convention in this unit. Have students read the unit introduction. Ask them to imagine that they are the Framers in Philadelphia. Discuss with them the following questions:

- What are some of the common ideas that you share about government?

- What experiences do you have in common?

- What differences separate you?

UNIT PROJECT (optional)

Review the definition of "Framers," those who participated in writing the Constitution. Point out that many other men and women contributed ideas that helped shape our Constitution. But the Framers were those delegates who actually attended the Philadelphia Convention in the summer of 1787.

In addition to the bulletin board display described on page 2 of the student text, you might wish to do an additional project with your students. Organize the class into small groups of 3-4 students and have each group select one delegate who attended the Philadelphia Convention. Groups may wish to select a delegate from the "Biographies of Important Framers" contained in the Reference Section of the student text. Alternatively, if they did the optional Unit One project, they might wish to study a Framer from the same state. Groups should try to obtain a portrait of their Framer and learn about his contribution to the convention. They should also try to find out their Framer's positions on the major conflicts examined in this unit.

How did the Philadelphia Convention begin?

LESSON OVERVIEW

This lesson looks at the men who attended the Philadelphia Convention, their backgrounds, and their goals. It also examines the decisions made by the delegates at the beginning of the convention.

The lesson opens with a problem-solving activity that asks students to consider how they would choose representatives to write a constitution for their student government. When students have completed this activity, they should be able to relate their answers to what actually happened at the Philadelphia Convention.

LESSON OBJECTIVES

At the conclusion of this lesson:

1. Students should be able to name some of the important Framers at the Philadelphia Convention and the role that each man played.

2. Students should be able to name some of the Founders not present in Philadelphia and explain their absence.

3. Students should be able to describe some of the agreements that the delegates made at the beginning of the Philadelphia Convention.

MATERIALS NEEDED

1. Student text

2. Handout 7-1 (optional)

TEACHING PROCEDURES

A. Introductory Activity:
Who should participate in creating a government?

Have the students read the "Purpose of Lesson." Then organize the class into groups of 3-5 students and have them read the problem-solving activity. Each group is to formulate answers to the questions and write its answers on chart paper or the chalkboard. Call on a member of each group to report its responses the rest of the class. Be sure to emphasis the last question, number 7, which allows the students to discuss the ideas of good government that they studied in Unit One.

B. Reading and Discussion:
Understanding who attended the convention

Assign students to read the sections "Who were the Framers?" and "Three important Framers." Review and list with the students common traits shared by the Framers. Ask them to consider why there were no women, blacks, or Native Americans at the convention. You may wish to have students discuss whether a convention that did not represent all segments of the population could write a constitution that would protect the rights of everyone.

C. Reading and Discussion:
Understanding who did not attend the Convention

Have students read the section, "Important Founders who were not at the convention." Discuss the reasons why many Founders refused to attend the convention. Ask the students if they think not attending the convention was the best way to oppose the writing of a new constitution.

D. Reading and Discussion:
Understanding initial decisions of the Framers

Have students read the section "The convention begins." Discuss with the students the four agreements made by the delegates. Ask the students if they think the Framers were justified in ignoring their instructions to amend the Articles of Confederation. Then discuss whether they think the Framers were correct in keeping the convention proceedings secret. You may wish to assign the third question in "Reviewing and using the lesson" at this time.

E. Concluding Activity

Conclude the lesson with a discussion of the questions in "Reviewing and using the lesson." Time might be given for students to work on their unit project. Students should also review the new terms in this lesson and add them to their vocabulary-building activity.

OPTIONAL ACTIVITIES

For Reinforcement, Extended Learning, and Enrichment

1. Have students role play, with partners, the job of a copy editor who must correct a reporter's story about the Philadelphia Convention. Distribute copies of Handout 7-1 and read aloud with the students the directions for the activity.

2. Have the students read *Sh! We're Writing the Constitution* by Jean Fritz (New York: Putnam, 1987) for a more detailed description of the Framers and the convention proceedings.

3. In 1787, fifty-five men attended the Philadelphia Convention, but the delegates did not represent large segments of the American population. Ask students to discuss whether they think it would be fair to have such a convention today .

Handout 7-1

What is wrong with this story?

Instructions:

The reporter who wrote the story below made some important mistakes. Based on what you have read in the text, underline the word (or group of words) that you think is incorrect. Count the number of mistakes you find. Compare your findings with those of your partner. Then work with your partner to rewrite the story correctly.

There were 105 delegates attending a constitutional convention held in Washington, D.C., in the winter of 1764. Most of the Framers were young men and women who were rich and important in their states. The delegates also included some free black men, slaves, and poor farmers. James Madison was one of the important delegates at the convention. George Washington also attended the convention—probably because he loved politics so much. Patrick Henry came too. He thought a strong national government was a great idea.

The first thing the Framers decided to do was ignore their instructions to just "fix" the Articles of Confederation. They decided that the best thing to do was to start over again and write a new constitution. Because this was such an important event, the Framers decided to call in the country's best reporters to make sure that history was well-recorded and that everyone would know about the convention right away.

How many representatives should each state have in Congress?

LESSON OVERVIEW

After reaching initial agreement on the conduct of the convention, the delegates soon ran into disagreements over a number of major issues. This lesson looks at the conflict over representation in the legislative branch of the new national government.

The lesson opens with a problem-solving activity that deals with the issue of representation. Students will also be able to look at population data from 1787 and think about the conflicting interests of the individual states based on their size. Students then examine the arguments on both sides of the conflict and discuss the compromise that finally solved this issue.

LESSON OBJECTIVES

At the conclusion of this lesson:

1. Students should be able to explain why representation was an issue at the convention.

2. Students should be able to explain the arguments of the small states and the large states on the issue of representation.

3. Students should be able to describe the key features of the Great Compromise.

MATERIALS NEEDED

1. Student text

2. Handout 8-1 (optional)

3. Handout 8-2 (optional)

TEACHING PROCEDURES

A. Introductory Activity:
How many representatives should your state have?

Have students read the "Purpose of Lesson." Then ask them to imagine that they are delegates to the Philadelphia Convention and are responsible for deciding how many representatives each state should be able to send to Congress. Follow the directions in the student text to conduct the problem-solving activity. Tell the students they are doing exactly what the Framers did at the convention: they are forming a committee made up of delegates from both large and small states to develop a solution to present to the rest of the convention.

B. Reading and Discussion:
Understanding the conflict between the large and small states

Have the students read "The conflict between the large and small states." Discuss the concerns of delegates from both the large and small states over representation in Congress. Students should examine the bar graph on page 60 and consider possible solutions that would meet the interests of all the states. At this point, you might wish to distribute copies of Handout 8-1 and have the students answer the questions based on the information provided in the graph. Explain that each segment on the graph represents 50,000 people.

C. Reading and Discussion:
Understanding the Great Compromise

Ask the students to read "The Great Compromise." Discuss the nature of compromise and how a compromise is reached. Then ask them to give examples from their own lives, of times they have needed to compromise. You might wish to distribute copies of Handout 8-2 and have the students think of possible compromises for the problem of the three brothers.

Explain to students that some of the compromises the Framers came up with were quite complicated. Write the main points of the Great Compromise on the chalkboard and ask them to look at the two scales on page 62. They should consider how the formula for representation in the Senate protects the interests of the states with small populations while the formula for representation in the House protects the interests of the large states.

D. Concluding Activity

Conclude the lesson by leading a discussion of the questions contained in "Reviewing and using the lesson." You might wish to assign questions 2 and 3 as homework and encourage the students to find newspaper articles about their senators and representatives. Students should also review the terms in the lesson and add them to their vocabulary lists.

OPTIONAL ACTIVITIES

For Reinforcement, Extended Learning, and Enrichment

1. Divide the class into unequal sized groups — one composed of only a few students and one composed of the majority of the class. Tell the groups that even though they are different sizes, they may only send one representative each to make a decision about how much free time the class will get that day. Discuss why this arrangement is fair or unfair.

2. Read aloud the chapter "The Melody Lingers On" from *55 Men: The Story of the Constitution* (Harrisburg, PA: Stackpole Books, 1986, originally published in 1936). This chapter discusses the issues covered in this lesson.

Handout 8-1

Population and representation

Use the bar graph in the lesson to complete the questions below. These questions will help you think about the conflict over representation.

1. Which state had the fewest people? _____

2. Which state had the most people? _____

3. If each state had one representative for every 50,000 people, how many representatives would each state have?

Connecticut	_____	New York	_____
Delaware	_____	North Carolina	_____
Georgia	_____	Pennsylvania	_____
Maryland	_____	Rhode Island	_____
Massachusetts	_____	South Carolina	_____
New Hampshire	_____	Virginia	_____

4. Which states do you think favored giving all states the same number of representatives?

5. Which states do you think favored giving the larger states more representatives based on the size of their populations?

6. What would be a fair solution to this problem?

Handout 8-2

How would you solve this problem?

Three brothers have inherited 15 acres from a rich uncle. They must decide how best to use the land. The first brother, a farmer, believes that the community needs more farm land to produce more crops. The second brother, an artist, believes that the community needs a beautiful park where families can spend time together. The third brother believes that a factory that would give jobs to people in the community would be the best way to use the land.

1. Can all three brothers get everything they want?

2. Can you think of any way that each of the three brothers gets at least part of what he wants?

If you thought of a solution, you thought of a **compromise**. A compromise is a solution in which each side gives up something and each side gets something.

How should the problem of slavery be handled?

LESSON OVERVIEW

This lesson deals with the controversy over slavery that divided the delegates from the Northern and Southern states. Students will read about the development of slavery in America and why it was more prevalent in the South than in the North. They will learn about the compromises over slavery that were made in order to convince Southern delegates to support the Constitution. They should understand that the compromises made at the convention did not solve the problem of slavery but were necessary to keep the nation together. Without these compromises, it was unlikely that a number of the Southern states would have agreed to support the Constitution.

LESSON OBJECTIVES

At the conclusion of this lesson:

1. Students should be able to explain why people in the North and South had different attitudes toward slavery.

2. Students should be able to describe the disagreements about slavery that confronted the Framers.

3. Students should be able to describe the compromises that were made at the convention to deal with the problem of slavery.

MATERIALS NEEDED

Student text

TEACHING PROCEDURES

A. Introductory Activity:
Understanding the nature of slavery in America

Have the students read the "Purpose of Lesson" and the section on "Slavery in America." Discuss with the students the characteristics of American slavery. Point out to the class that in 1787 there were slaves in the North as well as in the South. However, the South was already economically more dependent on slavery than was the rest of the nation.

B. Reading and Discussion:
Understanding the Framers' ideas about slavery

Assign students to read the section "What did the Framers think about slavery?" You may emphasize that many of the Framers were aware of the contradiction between the principles of natural rights and the institution of slavery. The problem at the convention was the need to balance the belief that slavery was wrong with the need to win the support of the delegates from the Southern states.

List for the students the three main problems about slavery that the Framers needed to solve. Explain the need for compromise and ask the students how they think the Framers might have solved these three issues.

C. Reading and Discussion:
Understanding the compromises on slavery

Have students read the section "What compromises did the Framers make?" Relate each of these compromises to one of the problems listed in the previous section. Make sure that students understand what the Northern and Southern states gave up and what they gained in the process of compromise. You may wish at this point to have students do the third activity listed in "Reviewing and using the lesson."

D. Reading and Discussion:
Understanding the end of slavery

Assign students to read the section "The end of slavery." You may wish to construct a timeline illustrating the following events in the history of slavery.

1619	first slaves brought to British colonies in America
1776	Declaration of Independence
1787	Philadelphia Convention
1860 - 1865	Civil War
1866	13th Amendment abolishes slavery

Point out to students that slavery continued in this country for almost 80 years after the Philadelphia Convention. Although many Americans objected to slavery, it became part of the economic way of life in much of the South. It took a civil war and much bloodshed to end slavery.

E. Concluding Activity

Conclude the lesson by discussing the questions contained in "Reviewing and using the lesson." Students may review the terms in the lesson and add them to their vocabulary-building activity. Time should also be given for students to work on their unit project.

OPTIONAL ACTIVITIES

For Reinforcement, Extended Learning, and Enrichment

1. Tell students they will be role-playing newspaper reporters interviewing Americans in 1787 about slavery. Divide the class into small groups. One group will play the role of newspaper reporters. The other groups will represent different points of view, both for and against slavery, such as: Southern slaveowner, Northern opponent of slavery, slave, Northern ship owner trading in slaves, and religious leader opposed to slavery. This activity can be performed as a skit and, if desired, a newspaper article may also be written.

2. Have students pretend to be newspaper editors. Ask them to write short editorials saying why it is "desirable" or "not desirable" to count each slave as three-fifths of a person.

Lesson 10

What basic ideas are in the Preamble to the Constitution?

LESSON OVERVIEW

This lesson explores some of the ideas in the Preamble to the Constitution. Students learn the importance of the words, "We the People ...." The lesson emphasizes that the power to govern belongs to the people who have created the government to protect their rights and promote their welfare. Students read the Preamble and develop definitions for the six key phrases in the document.

LESSON OBJECTIVES

At the conclusion of this lesson:

1. Students should be able to explain the purpose of the Preamble to the Constitution.

2. Students should be able to explain what some of the key phrases in the Preamble mean.

MATERIALS NEEDED

Student text

TEACHING PROCEDURES

A. Introductory Activity:
Understanding the importance of the Preamble

Have the students read the "Purpose of Lesson " and "What does the Preamble say?" Ask them why the first words of the Preamble are so important. Emphasize to the students that, in our country, the power of government belongs to the people.

B. Problem-solving Activity:
Understanding the Preamble's ideas

Have the students read "The Preamble's Ideas." Organize the class into six groups and assign each group one of the phrases from the Preamble. Follow the directions in the student text to conduct the problem-solving activity. Allow students to use dictionaries, encyclopedias, history books, and this text to help them in answering the three questions.

You may wish to have each group develop a skit which portrays its assigned phrase. Each group should present its skit and the rest of the class should guess which phrase of the Preamble is being portrayed. Each group should present its skit before it discusses its answers to the questions in the problem-solving activity.

In examining the Preamble to the Constitution, focus on the ideas that are contained in it rather than just the words themselves. You might wish to ask students how each illustration is related to the Preamble. Pay particular attention to the cartoon on "domestic tranquility." Ask the students to compare the idea in the cartoon with what the Framers actually meant when they wrote "insure domestic tranquility."

C. Concluding Activity

Conclude the lesson by discussing the questions in "Reviewing and using the lesson." Students might review the terms and add them to their vocabulary-building activity. Students should be completing their project for Unit Two.

OPTIONAL ACTIVITIES

For Reinforcement, Extended Learning, and Enrichment

1. Review with students why the Preamble was written. Ask them to write their own Preambles telling what they believe the purpose of government should be.

2. Have students do a comparison between the ideals of the Declaration of Independence and the Preamble to the Constitution. Assign students the following exercise.

   - Ask students to look at the section of the Declaration which is on page 41 of the student text. Have them review their own rewritten version of this document which they did earlier. Ask them to describe the purpose of the Declaration.

   - Ask students to reread the Preamble of the Constitution on page 71 of the student text and describe its purpose.

   - Ask students to describe the differences they see between the purposes of these two documents.

Students should be aware, as they have studied in Lesson 5, that the purpose of the Declaration was to justify the American revolt against Great Britain. The purpose of the Constitution was to establish the new government.

Unit Three

How did the Framers organize our government?

UNIT OVERVIEW

This unit of five lessons describes the way in which the Framers organized our national government. Students learn that one of the Framer's major concerns was to create a strong national government while, at the same time, limiting the powers of that government to protect the rights of the people. To do this, the Framers separated the powers of the national government into three branches. Students will study these three branches—the legislative, executive, and judicial—and learn how each can check the powers of the other so that no one branch can totally dominate the government. Students will also learn how the Framers created a federal system of government which further limited the power of the national government.

UNIT OBJECTIVES

At the conclusion of this unit:

1. Students should be able to define "separation of powers" and "checks and balances" and explain the reasons for each.

2. Students should be able to describe the powers and responsibilities of the legislative, executive, and judicial branches of our national government.

3. Students should be able to describe some of the ways in which the powers of each branch are limited.

4. Students should be able to explain what a federal system is and how powers are distributed in such a system.

UNIT INTRODUCTION

Ask students to look at the illustration at the beginning of the Unit Three introduction and have them explain its meaning. Discuss with the class the following questions:

- Who is the servant? Who is the master?

- Why is it important that government serves the people?

- How could the Framers make sure that the new government would serve the people?

Have students read the unit introduction. Tell them they will be learning how the Framers created some new and special ways to limit the powers of the national government so that it would serve the people.

Lesson 11

How did the Framers limit the powers of our government?

LESSON OVERVIEW

This lesson is designed to help students understand how the Framers wrote our Constitution to limit the powers of the national government. The lesson opens with a problem-solving activity that helps students think about how they would organize a government for their class. Students are then introduced to the concepts of separation of power and checks and balances. They learn that by dividing and balancing power between the three branches of government, and giving each branch a way to check on the power of the others, no one branch can completely control the government.

LESSON OBJECTIVES

At the conclusion of this lesson:

1. Students should be able to explain why the Framers thought it was necessary to limit the powers of the national government.

2. Students should be able to explain the concepts of separation of powers, balancing powers, and checking powers.

3. Students should be able to describe briefly the function of each of the branches of our government.

MATERIALS NEEDED

Student text

TEACHING PROCEDURES

A. Introductory Activity:
Organizing a class government

Have students read the "Purpose of Lesson." Then organize the class into groups of 3-5 students and have them read the problem-solving activity. Each group is to formulate answers to the questions and share its answers with the rest of the class. You might wish to extend the discussion by analyzing your school and/or class government. Students should be encouraged to think about how power is limited when it is shared by different groups. They should be asked why it is necessary to limit the power of government. Students should remember that one of the key characteristics of a constitutional government is that its powers are limited.

B. Reading and Discussion:
Introducing some new concepts

Have the students read aloud "What ideas did the Framers use?" Write the terms "separation of powers" and "checks and balances" on the chalkboard and tell the class that these are the important ideas they will be studying. The students should be able to draw some parallels between the ideas they presented during the problem-solving activity and the ideas of the Framers.

C. Reading and Discussion:
Understanding separation of powers

Ask students to read "Separation of powers" and then write on the chalkboard or on chart paper the terms "Legislative branch," "Executive branch," and "Judicial branch." Review with students the functions of each of these branches. Ask them why they think the Framers chose to divide power among these three branches.

D. Reading and Discussion:
Understanding the balancing and checking of powers

Have students read "Balancing powers," "Checking powers," and "Why did the Framers organize our government this way?" Explain that separation of powers alone is not sufficient to limit the power of the government. Balances and checks allow each branch of the government to limit the power of the other branches. You may wish to use the illustration on page 79 to allow students to think of a constitutional government as one in which all branches are balanced on a three-part scale. Remind students that when the scale is out of balance, a government can gain too much power. When this happens, the rights of the people may no longer be protected.

E. Concluding Activity

Conclude the lesson with a discussion of the questions in "Reviewing and using the lesson." Time might be given for students to work on their bulletin board display. Students should also review the new terms in the lesson and add them to their vocabulary-building activity.

OPTIONAL ACTIVITIES

For Reinforcement, Extended Learning, and Enrichment

1. Have students look in newspapers and newsmagazines for examples of one branch of government checking the use of power by another.

2. Invite a local public official to visit your class and talk about how the principles of separation of powers and checks and balances are embodied in your local government.

Lesson 12

What is the legislative branch?

LESSON OVERVIEW

This lesson examines the legislative branch of government in a way that requires student involvement, creative decision-making, and analysis of a "real-life" situation.

Students first read the text, examining the organization of the two houses of Congress, the powers of Congress, and the procedures for making a law. Students then read about the responsibilities of a representative. They are presented with a dilemma on how a senator should vote when faced with a conflict between the common good and the economic needs of her particular state. Students complete their reading by considering the limitations on the power of Congress.

LESSON OBJECTIVES

At the conclusion of this lesson:

1. Students should be able to explain the function of the legislative branch.

2. Students should be able to describe the procedure for making a law.

3. Students should be able to describe the powers of Congress and the limitations on those powers.

MATERIALS NEEDED

1. Student text

2. Handouts 12-1 and 12-2 (optional)

TEACHING PROCEDURES

A. Introductory Activity:
Identifying our national legislature

Introduce this lesson by asking students what they know about the legislative branch of government. Write their ideas on the chalkboard to compare their findings with what they read in the lesson. Then have the students read the "Purpose of Lesson" and "What is Congress?"

B. Reading and Discussion:
Understanding how Congress works

Have the students read the section "What are the powers of Congress?" You may wish to refer students to Article I, Section 8 of the Constitution and review some of the powers of Congress listed there. Students should also review what they have studied about "general welfare" in Lesson 10 and apply this concept to the power of Congress to promote the general welfare.

Students should then read "How does Congress make a law?" Review with them the three steps described and discuss the difference between a bill and a law.

C. Problem Solving:
How should Senator Smith vote?

Have students read "What are the responsibilities of your members of Congress?" Discuss with the students how members of Congress can respond to the needs of their constituents. Students should be encouraged to think about the following questions:

- What happens when constituent needs conflict with what a member of Congress believes to be right?

- What happens when constituent needs conflict with the common welfare?

Read orally with the students the instructions for the problem-solving activity, "How should Senator Smith vote?" Divide the class into groups of 3-5 students. One group should represent Senator Smith and her staff. The other groups should represent people in Senator Smith's state and could include such divergent groups as tobacco farmers, cigarette factory owners, smokers, nonsmokers, representatives of health organizations, environmentalists, and restaurant owners.

Groups will need to discuss the problem and develop a position based on their roles. All members should be ready to present their proposals to the class.

D. Reading and Discussion:
Understanding the limits on congressional power

Have the students read "How are the powers of Congress limited?" Point out to the class that the two major ways to limit the powers of Congress are the veto power of the President and the power of the Supreme Court to declare a law unconstitutional. Remind students that these limits are part of the system of checks and balances they studied in Lesson 11.

E. Concluding Activity

Conclude the lesson by discussing the questions in "Reviewing and using the lesson." The first two questions provide an opportunity for students to become familiar with the actual language of the Constitution at a level they can understand. Students should review the new terms and include them in their vocabulary-building activity.

OPTIONAL ACTIVITIES

For Reinforcement, Extended Learning, and Enrichment

1. Have students do individual research on their senator or representative. This could include writing to their member of Congress and collecting news articles about him or her.

2 Provide students with copies of three or four hand-picked newspaper articles. Have them search for examples of actions by Congress, underlining names of the members of Congress and the legislation discussed in the articles.

3. Have a staff member from the local office of your member of Congress talk to the class about the responsibilities of their representative or senator.

4. Divide the class into small groups to discuss and present answers to the questions posed in Handouts 12-1 and 12-2. Students could, if desired, act as delegates to the Philadelphia Convention considering the qualifications and length of service of members of Congress.

Handout 12-1

Who should be in the Congress?

A. How old should a senator or a representative be?

  1. Should there be a minimum age to be in Congress? Support your position.

  2. Should senators and representatives have the same minimum age? Support your position.

  3. If not, which position should have the older age? Why? How much older?

  4. Should the person be old enough to finish high school? college? Why?

  5. Should the person be old enough to have married? have a family? have grown children? Why?

  6. Should the person be old enough to have started their own business or farm? or have become a master at their craft? Why?

B. Should a senator or a representative have to live in the state that they will represent?

  1. Should persons who wish to be senators or representatives be citizens of the U.S.? Should these individuals be citizens of the states that they will represent? Why?

  2. Should these persons have to live inside the state for a length of time before they are selected to be a senator or a representative? If so, why and for how long?

Handout 12-2

How long should the Congress serve?

A. How long should the terms of office be?

    1. Should the senators and representatives have the same length of service? Why?

    2. If not, which should serve the longer term? Why?

    3. Should the years of service be odd years (1,3,5 years) or even years (2,4,6 years)? Why?

B. Can a senator or a representative be re-elected?

    1. What are the good points in allowing re-election?

    2. What are the bad points in allowing re-election?

    3. Should there be a limited number of times a member of Congress can be re-elected? Why?

C. When should senators and representatives be selected?

    1. What are the advantages and disadvantages of having both the senators and representatives elected at the same time?

    2. What are the advantages and disadvantages of having the senators and representatives elected for different periods of time?

Lesson 13

What is the executive branch?

LESSON OVERVIEW

This lesson introduces students to the executive branch of our national government. They learn about the concerns of the Framers in balancing the need for an effective president with the fear of giving too much power to one person. Students will be able to see how the powers of the Presidency are limited by Congress. They then read a story about our first President which emphasizes that our government is based on the consent of the people. The lesson concludes with an examination of how the first Congress organized the executive branch.

LESSON OBJECTIVES

At the conclusion of this lesson:

1. Students should be able to explain the concerns of the Framers when they created the executive branch.

2. Students should be able to describe the powers of the President.

3. Students should be able to describe the ways in which Congress limits the President's powers.

MATERIALS NEEDED

1. Student text

2. Handouts 13-1 and 13-2 (optional)

TEACHING PROCEDURES

A. Opening Activity:
Understanding the Framers' fears about a strong President

Have students read the "Purpose of Lesson" and "Creating the executive branch." Ask the students why the Framers were so afraid of a strong president. Discuss with them the colonial experiences with the British king. You may wish to review the American complaints against King George III contained in the Declaration of Independence (discussed in Lesson 5).

B. Reading and Discussion:
Understanding the powers of the President

Have the students read "What are the powers of the President?" and "How are the powers of the President limited by Congress?" Review these sections and outline on the board the ways in which Congress can limit the President's powers. Remind students that these limits are part of the system of checks and balances they have studied.

C. Reading and Discussion:
Considering Washington's role as our first President

Have students read "George Washington was our first President." Discuss with students the uniqueness of the Presidency in 1789. Have them imagine what it would be like to live in a world ruled by kings and then to meet a ruler whose power came from the people. Emphasize that the President's role was to serve the people, not to rule them.

Students should then read the story "Peter and President Washington" and answer the questions that follow.

D. Reading and Discussion:
Understanding the organization of the executive branch

Have students read "How is the executive branch organized?" You may wish to distribute copies of Handout 13-1 and have students discuss how the executive branch has grown since Washington was President. Students could be asked to collect news articles dealing with one or more of the cabinet members.

E. Concluding Activity

Conclude the lesson by having students discuss the questions in "Reviewing and using the lesson." Remind them to review the new terms in the lesson.

OPTIONAL ACTIVITIES

For Reinforcement, Extended Learning, and Enrichment

1 Have students write a job description or want ad for the Presidency.

2. Have students watch the newspaper each day for political cartoons about the President. What are the cartoonists trying to say about the President? Is the media coverage of the President fair? Why or why not?

3. Have students research to find if any of the Presidents of the United States have ever been impeached and for what reason. Use this information to write a report.

4. Divide the class into five groups and tell the students they will act as delegates to the Philadelphia Convention creating the office of President. Distribute Handout 13-2 and assign each group one of the questions in the Handout. Each group is to formulate answers to the question it has been assigned and report its answers to the rest of the class.

THE EXECUTIVE BRANCH

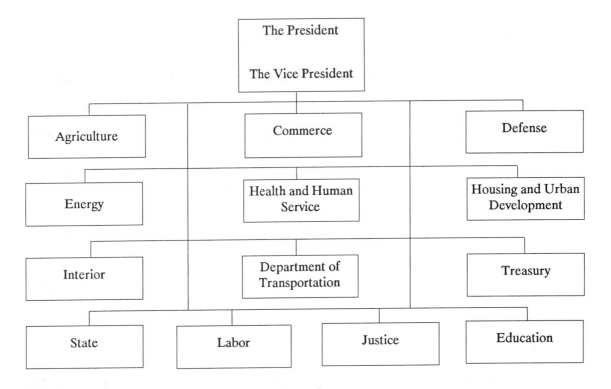

Handout 13-2

Creating the Presidency

1. How old should the President be?

    a. What are the good and bad points of having a young person (under the age of 35) as President?

    b. What are the good and bad points of having an older person (older than 35) as President?

2. Should the President be a citizen of the United States?

    a. What are the good and bad points of a President who was born in the U.S.?

    b. What are the good and bad points of a President who was born in another country?

3. What should the term of office be for the Presidency?

    a. What would be the good and bad points of choosing a new President every two years?

    b. What would be the good and bad points of having a longer term of four years?

4. Can a President be re-elected?

    a. What are the good and bad points of allowing a person to be re-elected to the Presidency?

    b. What are the good and bad points of putting a limit on the number of times a persons can be re-elected?

5. How many chief executives should there be?

    a. What are the good and bad points of having one President?

    b. What are the good and bad point of having more than one President?

Lesson 14

What is the judicial branch?

LESSON OVERVIEW

This lesson examines the judicial branch and the power of judicial review. Students learn that the courts protect the rights of the people against any unconstitutional actions by the President or Congress. The power of judicial review is an important check by the judiciary on the other two branches of government. Students will read about an actual case, *Torcaso v. Watkins*, to see how the Supreme Court used its power of judicial review to strike down an unconstitutional state law.

LESSON OBJECTIVES

At the conclusion of this lesson:

1. Students should be able to describe the functions of the judicial branch.

2. Students should be able to explain how members of the judiciary are selected.

3. Students should be able to define judicial review and explain its importance.

MATERIALS NEEDED

Student text

TEACHING PROCEDURES

A. Introductory Activity:
Understanding the role of the judicial branch

Read aloud to the class the following excerpt from the Constitution: "Congress shall have Power ... [to] provide for the ... general welfare of the United States." Ask students if the meaning of this phrase is clear. Why might people argue about what it means? Who should decide what the words in the Constitution mean?

Explain that one of the functions of the judicial branch is to settle disputes about what the Constitution and the federal laws mean. Have students read the "Purpose of Lesson" and "What does the judicial branch do?" Discuss with the class the role of the courts.

B. Reading and Discussion:
Understanding the organization of the judicial branch

Have the class read "How is the judicial branch organized?" Ask students whether they agree that judges should be appointed rather than elected. You might wish to discuss the third question in "Reviewing and using the lesson" at this time. The issue is whether judges, who are appointed, should have the power to overrule the will of the majority as expressed by elected representatives.

C. Reading and Discussion:
Understanding judicial review

Have students read the last two sections in the lesson. Discuss the meaning of judicial review and remind students of its importance in protecting our constitutional rights. Judicial review allows people, especially minorities, to seek protection of rights that government agencies have attempted to limit. The case of *Torcaso v. Watkins* provides students with an opportunity to see how the Supreme Court used its power of judicial review to protect religious freedom. Students will learn more about how the courts protect our rights in Unit Four.

D. Concluding Activity

Conclude the lesson with a discussion of the questions in "Reviewing and using the lesson." Students should be given an opportunity to work on their bulletin board display. Students should also add the new terms in this lesson to their vocabulary-building activity.

OPTIONAL ACTIVITIES

For Reinforcement, Extended Learning, and Enrichment

1 Have individual students research the lives and careers of famous justices on the U.S. Supreme Court.

2. Interested students could write a proposal for a student court at your school. They would need to decide what types of cases they would hear, the extent of punishment they would recommend to the principal, the procedures in the student court, and the selection of the student judges.

What is a federal government?

LESSON OVERVIEW

This lesson is intended to introduce students to our federal system of government. It opens with a problem-solving activity that allows students to explore visually the origins and distribution of power within our federal system. Students are then given examples of how federalism works. They learn that in the inevitable conflicts between the state and federal government, the authority of the Constitution is superior to the power of the state. The lesson concludes with an introduction to the Bill of Rights which students will study in greater depth in Unit Four.

LESSON OBJECTIVES

At the conclusion of this lesson:

1. Students should be able to explain the concept of a federal system of government.

2. Students should be able to give examples of how powers are distributed in the federal system.

3. Students should be able to describe reasons why the Framers created this new system of government.

MATERIALS NEEDED

Student text

TEACHING PROCEDURES

A. Introductory Activity:
Understanding a federal system of government

Introduce the lesson by referring to the concept of sovereignty discussed in Lesson 10. Remind students that the power of government belongs to the people. When the Framers wrote our Constitution, they were concerned about how to distribute this power. How much power should be given to the national government? How much should be retained by the states and by the people?

Have students read the "Purpose of Lesson." Then read aloud with the class the introduction to the problem-solving activity and refer them to the illustration on page 100. After students have had an opportunity to answer the questions in the problem-solving activity, they should share their answers with the class. Students should be encouraged to discuss the last question, "Why do you think the Framers chose this system of government?"

B. Reading and Discussion:
Understanding the division of powers

Have the students read "Where have the people placed the power?" and "The powers of the federal government are greater than those of the state." Be certain they understand the different types of power given to the federal and state governments. They should know that when there is a conflict, the power of the federal government is greater than that of the state governments.

C. Reading and Discussion:
Understanding the need for a bill of rights

Have students read the last section "Limiting government to protect our rights." Ask students why they think the Framers wanted to divide the power of government between the federal and state governments. Would such a division of powers be enough to protect the rights of the people? Remind the class that many of the Founders were suspicious of a strong national government. These people refused to support the Constitution unless there was a written guarantee of the individual rights of the people. Many state constitutions already contained such guarantees. The supporters of the Constitution promised to pass a bill of rights during the first Congress. The Bill of Rights, like checks and balances and the federal system, was another limitation on the power of the national government and was meant to protect the rights of the people.

D. Concluding Activity

Discuss with students the questions in "Reviewing and using the lesson." Have students add the new terms in the lesson to their vocabulary-building activity. You might wish to allow time for students to complete their bulletin board display for Unit Three.

OPTIONAL ACTIVITIES

For Reinforcement, Extended Learning, and Enrichment

1. Most laws that affect us directly are state laws. Have students keep track of their actions and activities for one school day. How were their actions or activities affected by laws? How many are federal laws? State laws? Local laws?

2. Have students check news articles for examples of issues that illustrate the division of power between the state and federal governments. Have them make a bulletin board display showing these issues.

Unit Four

How does the Constitution protect your basic rights?

UNIT OVERVIEW

This unit explains how the Bill of Rights came to be adopted, and looks at five basic rights protected under the Constitution: freedom of expression, freedom of religion, equal protection, due process, and the right to vote. The lessons discuss the importance of these rights, and examine situations in which issues have been raised with regard to their interpretation. Lesson 18, on equal protection, focuses on the changes made by the Supreme Court in interpreting the equal protection clause, which have extended the right to equal protection to groups denied that protection in the past. Lesson 20, on the right to vote, focuses on the expansion of that right by amendments to the Constitution.

UNIT OBJECTIVES

At the conclusion of this unit:

1. Students should be able to explain what the Bill of Rights is, why it was added to the Constitution, and how it now applies to actions of either the national or state governments.

2. Students should be able to name and explain the meaning of five key rights which are guaranteed by the Constitution: to free expression, religious freedom, equal protection of the law, due process of law, and the vote.

3. Students should be able to explain the importance of these rights to a democratic society.

UNIT INTRODUCTION

Read the text of the unit introduction with the class. Make sure they understand that the rights they will be studying are (through amendments and interpretations by the Supreme Court) protected from infringement by national, state, and local governments.

UNIT PROJECT (optional)

In addition to the bulletin board display described on page 2 of the student text, you might assign partners to work together on a unit project, a collage. You can assign each group to focus on one of the rights in the unit or allow them to cover all five rights on their collage. You will need to collect old magazines and newspapers ahead of time. Provide the groups with a folder or envelope to store their clippings and a box in the room where these folders/envelopes can be kept.

How does the Constitution protect your freedom of expression?

LESSON OVERVIEW

When the Founders chose to amend the Constitution through the addition of the Bill of Rights, they placed in the First Amendment the right to freedom of expression. Some scholars argue that this indicates the importance the Founders placed upon this freedom. In this lesson, students will first read sections dealing with the forms of expression protected by the Constitution, the benefits resulting from freedom of expression, and the need to protect this right. The lesson ends with a problem-solving activity that explores the limits to free expression.

LESSON OBJECTIVES

At the conclusion of the lesson:

1. Students should be able to state the various forms of expression covered by the First Amendment.

2. Students should be able to describe the benefits of freedom of expression to the individual and to a democratic society.

3. Students should be able to discuss and explain what they might consider reasonable limits on freedom of expression.

MATERIALS NEEDED

Student text

TEACHING PROCEDURES

A. Introductory Activity:
Exploring the meaning of expression

Write the word "expression" on the chalkboard, and explore with your students its meaning. Brainstorm with them the various ways students express themselves through actions, speech, songs, word games, art, movement, writing, attires, etc.

B. Reading and Discussion:
Identifying freedom of expression

Ask students to read the "Purpose of Lesson" and "What is freedom of expression?" Review with them the four forms of freedom of expression. You might wish to explore with them derivative forms of speech—for example, buttons, attire with slogans, protest signs, and picketing.

C. Reading and Discussion:
Understanding the benefits of freedom of expression

Assign students to read the sections "What are the benefits of freedom of expression?" and "Why is it necessary to protect freedom of expression?" Review with them the four benefits of freedom of expression and historical incidents of intolerance toward free expression. (A famous example is Galileo, who was forced to recant his view that the earth was not the center of the universe but instead moved around the sun.)

You might wish to explore with them some of the possible costs of free expression that is unpopular — public disapproval, job loss, disruptive demonstrations, etc. — and balance these costs, some to the individual and some to the public, against the benefits enumerated.

D. Reading and Discussion:
Discovering the limits to freedom of expression

Have the students read the section, "Should freedom of expression ever be limited?" Review with them the two examples given, then explore with them other possible situations where limits might be placed on expression. Possible situations might be:

- One student dislikes another in his class. He calls the other student offensive names whenever he has the chance. Should offensive names be protected by freedom of expression?

- A rock band practices at 2 a.m. out in the backyard or in the local neighborhood park. Is it reasonable to limit this "freedom of expression"? Is there a better time or location to practice?

- The student newspaper prints lies and rumors about a student. Do the student reporters have a responsibility to tell the truth? Should they print both sides to a story? Should they be stopped from printing lies?

- A group of students are angry at a store in the mall, which refuses to hire nonwhites as clerks. After being unsuccessful in persuading the store management to change its policy, they protest by sitting down in the middle of the shopping mall and at all entrances to the store. They also carry signs that explain their complaints. Their action effectively prevents business from being conducted. Is this a reasonable way to express their protest? What other steps could they have taken?

- A group of students protests the bad food in the cafeteria by starting a food fight. Is this a reasonable way to express an opinion about the quality of the food? What else could the students have done?

E. Problem Solving:
When should freedom of expression be limited?

Organize the class into groups of 2-3 students and ask them to read through the problem-solving activity. Have them write out a group answer to the four questions on either binder paper or chart paper. Each group will then choose one member to present the group's answers to the class.

F. Concluding Activity

Conclude the lesson by leading a discussion of the questions contained in "Reviewing and using the lesson." If the students have been assigned the unit project, have the groups begin collecting clippings for their collages. Encourage them to group the clippings according to the right being illustrated.

OPTIONAL ACTIVITIES

For Reinforcement, Extended Learning, and Enrichment

1. Students might debate the issue of the motion picture ratings system that limits the movies that young persons can view, or the issue of a proposed rating system for rock music recordings.

2. Invite a local law enforcement official or lawyer to speak on local guidelines regarding public demonstrations.

3. Invite representatives from local newspapers, television, or radio stations to speak to the class on limits that the government places on freedom of expression in their fields. Students could also examine the limits placed on expression in student-run newspapers and other publications.

How does the Constitution protect your freedom of religion?

LESSON OVERVIEW

The Founders placed freedom of religion with freedom of expression in the First Amendment. However, the religion clauses precede the expression clauses. Some constitutional experts believe that this placement indicates the primary emphasis the Founders placed on protecting religious freedom.

Students read sections on the meaning of freedom of religion, its importance to the Founders, and on the conflicts over the interpretation of the freedom of religion clauses. Students then engage in a problem-solving activity that looks at the issue of prayer in the public schools. The lesson ends with sections that examine the distinction between limiting religious beliefs and limiting religious practices.

LESSON OBJECTIVES

At the conclusion of this lesson:

1. Students should be able to explain the meaning of the freedom of religion clauses in the Constitution.

2. Students should be able to explain why the Founders placed so much importance on protecting freedom of religion.

3. Students should understand that there are conflicts over the interpretation of the freedom of religion clauses, particularly in some situations involving the issue of prayer in the public schools.

4. Students should be able to explain that, while religious belief may not be restricted, religious practices may be prohibited if they are harmful to public health or the common welfare.

MATERIALS NEEDED

Student text

TEACHING PROCEDURES

A. Introductory Activity:
Understanding the meaning of freedom of religion

Write the words "freedom of religion" on the board or chartpaper. Ask the class to brainstorm what that phrase means. List all the possibilities.

Now have the class read the sections "Purpose of Lesson" and "The First Amendment protects freedom of religion." Review with the students the meanings of the freedom-of-religion clauses in the Constitution. Compare these meanings with the ideas of the class.

B. Reading and Discussion:
Understanding the importance of religious freedom

Have students read the section "Why was freedom of religion so important to the Founders?" Ask the class why the Founders thought it was important to protect religious freedom. You might wish to discuss modern instances of religious persecution, such as the treatment of Jews in Nazi Germany.

C. Reading and Problem Solving:
Understanding conflicts involving freedom of religion

Organize the class into groups of 3-5 students. Have groups read the section "Conflicts over the freedom-of-religion clauses" and the problem-solving activity " Prayer in the public schools." Each group should prepare answers to the four questions and choose a spokesperson to report its findings to the rest of the class.

D. Reading and Discussion:
Understanding limits on religious freedom

Assign students the last two sections. Emphasize to the students that the government has no power to interfere with their right to believe in a religion of their own choosing, or not to believe in any religion at all.

Then make clear to the students that in some cases the practice of religion may be limited if that practice conflicts with the common welfare, public morality, or with the health and safety of others. Some issues that have arisen in this regard that might form the basis of a class debate are the following:

- Some churches do not believe in using modern medicine. Their church members refuse to allow their children to receive medication that could possibly cure their illnesses. Should the state step in, over the parents' wishes, to see that the child receives the medical help that has been recommended by doctors?

- Some churches use wine during the communion services. When children participate in these religious practices, they are in violation of state drinking laws that set the drinking age at 21 years or older. Should the state intervene and forbid the use of wine in these ceremonies?

- Some churches do not believe in using modern technology, bright colors, or symbolic signs. Their members refuse to attach bright reflector signs on the back of their buggies, so that they can be seen at night. Should the state step in and require the rear reflectors?

It is important for the students to understand the problem of balancing the right of the religious community to practice its beliefs and the right of the entire community to protect the health and safety of its members and to enforce the prevailing standards of morality.

E. Concluding Activity

Have the students participate in a discussion of answers to the questions under "Reviewing and using the lesson." Provide time for students to collect more clippings for their collages. Set a date for collecting the collages.

OPTIONAL ACTIVITIES

For Reinforcement, Extended Learning, and Enrichment

1. Students might do individual reports on some of the early religious dissenters such as Roger and Mary Williams, Anne Hutchinson, or Thomas Hooker.

2. Students might do a survey of their parents and adult community members, to determine if prayers were ever said in public school classrooms when they were students—and if so, under what circumstances. Students might also examine their own school experiences to determine if there have been times when prayers have been said—and if so, under what circumstances.

How does the Constitution protect your right to be treated equally by the government?

LESSON OVERVIEW

It was not until the 14th Amendment was added after the Civil War that the concept of equality gained a legal foothold in the Constitution. The equal protection clause finally incorporated in the Constitution the ideal that "all men are created equal," an ideal stated in the Declaration of Independence that had inspired so many during the American Revolution.

In this lesson, students will first participate in a problem-solving activity that examines problems involving inequality of treatment under state and local laws. They will then read and discuss sections explaining the Fourteenth Amendment's equal protection clause, its original interpretation by the Supreme Court, and the change in its interpretation by the Supreme Court in the famous case of *Brown v. Board of Education*. The lesson ends with a brief discussion of attempts to stop other forms of racial discrimination, as well as discrimination against other groups.

LESSON OBJECTIVES

At the conclusion of the lesson:

1. Students should be able to describe the equal protection clause and the changes in its interpretation that have helped to insure equal treatment of all citizens by government.

2. Students should be able to describe the case of *Brown v. Board of Education* and explain its importance in promoting equal protection of the law for all people under the Constitution.

MATERIALS NEEDED

Student text

TEACHING PROCEDURES

A. Introductory Activity:
Examining issues of equal treatment

Organize the class into groups of 3-5 students. Have the groups read the "Purpose of Lesson" and the problem-solving activity, "What is equal treatment?" Each group will study and discuss the five situations in this activity. They should develop answers for each situation. Ask each group to be ready to share its ideas with the rest of the class. Be sure that the students give the reasons for their answers.

B. Reading and Discussion:
Understanding the equal protection clause

Ask students to read the section "The Fourteenth Amendment and equal protection." Discuss with students the purpose of the Amendment. Point out that at first the Amendment did not accomplish its purpose, and discrimination against blacks continued. Nor did the original interpretation of the equal protection clause by the Supreme Court help. (In the case of *Plessy v. Ferguson* in 1896, the Court held that there was no violation of equal protection if public facilities were "separate but equal.") It was not until 1954, after World War II and in a different climate of public opinion, that the Supreme Court overruled its previous decision.

C. Reading and Discussion:
Understanding the importance of the *Brown* case

Assign students to read the sections, "What is the importance of the case of *Brown v. Board of Education*?" and "Ending Discrimination." Discuss the importance of the Court's change in interpreting the equal protection clause.

Emphasize to the students that separation or segregation in itself implies inequality and is unfair. As the Supreme Court said in its decision:

> To separate [children] from others of similar age and qualifications solely because of their race generates a feeling of inferiority as to their status in the community that may affect their hearts and minds in a way unlikely ever to be undone....Whatever may have been the extent of psychological knowledge at the time of *Plessy v. Ferguson*, this finding is amply supported by modern authority....Any language in *Plessy v. Ferguson* contrary to this finding is rejected....Separate educational facilities are inherently unequal....[We] hold that the plaintiffs...[are] deprived of the equal protection of the laws guaranteed by the Fourteenth Amendment.

D. Concluding Activity

Have students answer the questions under "Reviewing and using the lesson." Provide time for the students to work on their collages. They should begin thinking about the placement of the pictures on the posterboard.

OPTIONAL ACTIVITIES

For Reinforcement, Extended Learning, and Enrichment

1. Conduct a class discussion of the following questions: Are there some circumstances where it might be reasonable and fair to treat a particular group or class of people differently from others? For example, would it violate the principle of equal protection to refuse driving licenses to persons under 16 years of age in order to protect the safety of the public? Would it be reasonable to distinguish between girls and boys in this situation? Would restricting machine shop classes to boys violate the principle of equal protection of the laws?

2. Some schools divide their playgrounds and lunch periods by grade levels: 1st-3rd graders and 4th-6th graders. Discuss with students the fairness of this division. Are all the students being treated equally in this situation? Are there good and fair reasons for this division of students? Other examples to discuss might be: Should 6th graders be the only ones allowed to participate in student council, instrumental or choral music activities, or intramural sports?

3. Assign individual students to research reports about the civil rights struggles of blacks, Native Americans, Asians, women, and Hispanics.

How does the Constitution protect your right to be treated fairly by the government?

LESSON OVERVIEW

One of the great fears of the Founders and Framers was the tendency of powerful governments to act unfairly and unreasonably. The due process clause in the Fifth Amendment was intended by the Framers to prevent such abuse of power on the part of the federal government.

The due process clause in the Fourteenth Amendment protects against state or local government abuse of power. This clause has been interpreted by the courts to extend most of the rights in the Bill of Rights, that originally applied only to the federal government, to protect people against unfair actions by state and local governments.

Students first read about what due process means. Then they are involved in a problem-solving activity that raises questions about who should have the right to a lawyer in a criminal case. The lesson ends with a discussion of the importance of the right to due process in criminal proceedings, and of other situations in which the right to due process applies.

LESSON OBJECTIVES

At the conclusion of the lesson:

1. Students should be able to state in general terms what due process means.

2. Students should be able to explain the importance of the due process clauses in the Bill of Rights and the Fourteenth Amendment.

3. Students should be able to identify situations in which due process rights are important, particularly the right to a lawyer in criminal proceedings.

MATERIALS NEEDED

1. Student text

2. Handout 19-1 (optional)

TEACHING PROCEDURES

A. Introductory Activity:
Defining due process of law

Ask students to read the "Purpose of Lesson" and "What is due process of law?" Go over with them the location of the two due process clauses and the meaning of the phrase.

B. Problem Solving:
Determining who has the right to a lawyer

Form groups of 3-5 students and assign them the task of reading the problem-solving activity and answering the questions that follow. You might have students write their answers on chartpaper and share their opinions with the rest of the class.

Note: In the case of *Gideon v. Wainwright*, 372 U.S. 335 (1963), the Supreme Court overruled its decision in a case decided twenty years earlier, and held that a state must provide counsel for an indigent accused of a serious crime. This case is an example of how ideas as to what constitutes due process, or fundamental fairness, can change over time.

C. Reading and Discussion:
Understanding the importance of due process in criminal trials

Ask pairs of students to read the sections, "Why is due process important in criminal trials?" and "Other examples of due process rights." They should discuss and answer the questions that follow the first section. Also ask them to write down examples of rights to due process that would be important to school children.

D. Concluding Activity

Have the students answer the questions under "Reviewing and using the lesson." Remind the students of the due date on the collages. Allow time for work on the collages.

OPTIONAL ACTIVITIES

For Reinforcement, Extended Learning, and Enrichment

1. Point out that the public gets much of its information about due process from television programs. Have students watch some currently popular television series about police work, taking notes on procedures followed. Ask the students what they would have done in the situations portrayed. What actions by the police officers were fair or unfair? Then invite a police officer to visit the class and analyze the accuracy of the information conveyed on television.

2. Arrange to have the class visit and observe procedures at a local court hearing. If possible, have the judge discuss procedures with students.

3. A handout has been included for teachers who wish to extend students' knowledge of specific rights included in the Bill of Rights which are applicable to state actions under the due process clause of the Fourteenth Amendment. Distribute Handout 19-1 and allow time for students to complete the worksheet.

Handout 19-1

What rights do people have when they are suspected or accused of crimes?

Instructions: Read the protections in the Bill of Rights that are summarized below. Then answer the questions that follow.

Fourth Amendment:

- People, their homes, and their possessions cannot be searched or taken by the government without a good reason.
- In most cases, the police must get a warrant (permission from a judge) before they can conduct a search.

Fifth Amendment:

- People who are accused of crimes do not have to give evidence against themselves.
- People cannot be tried again for a crime for which they have been found innocent.
- People's lives, liberty, or property cannot be taken from them without due process of law.

Sixth Amendment:

- A person accused of a crime has the right to a speedy, public trial by a jury (other citizens).
- People must be told what crimes they are accused of.
- People have a right to question the persons who are accusing them.
- An accused person has the right to have a lawyer.

Eighth Amendment:

- People arrested for crimes are entitled to be free on reasonable bail (money deposited with the court) while awaiting trial.
- If a person must pay a fine, it must be a fair amount.
- People found guilty of crimes shall not be punished in cruel and unusual ways.

Suppose the police think you have committed a crime and come to arrest you. Which of the rights you have just read about do you think would be most important to you? Why?

How does the Constitution protect your right to vote?

LESSON OVERVIEW

This lesson focuses on the expansion of voting rights to groups who had originally been denied the right to vote. It discusses the elimination of barriers to voting by blacks, the achievement of woman suffrage, and the extension of the vote to Native Americans and eighteen-year-olds. It points out the discrepancy between the number of women voters and the number of women holding legislative or executive positions in the national government. It also points out the failure by many citizens between the ages of eighteen and twenty-one to use their right to vote.

LESSON OBJECTIVES

At the conclusion of this lesson:

1. Students should be able to describe steps taken to remove barriers to voting by blacks, to gain voting rights for women, and to extend the vote to Native Americans and to citizens over eighteen years of age.

2. Students should be able to describe voting requirements that are still left to the prerogative of the individual states.

MATERIALS NEEDED

1. Student text

2. Handout 20-1

3. Handout 20-2 (optional)

TEACHING PROCEDURES

A. Introductory Activity:
Identifying voting qualifications

Have students read the "Purpose of Lesson." Then organize the class into groups of 3-5 students and have them discuss and answer the two questions in the problem-solving activity "Who should have the right to vote?" Members of each group should be prepared to give the group's opinions to the rest of the class. After the group reports, have the class vote on their different suggestions as to who should have the right to vote.

B. Reading and Discussion:
Discovering early voting limitations

Have the class read "Early limits on the right to vote." Speculate with the class as to possible answers to the following questions:

- Why was voting limited to just men? What might have been the reasons for excluding women?

- Why was voting limited to just whites? What might have been the reasons for excluding non-white groups — blacks or Native Americans?

- Would property holders be better voters than non-landowners? Why or why not?

C. Reading and Discussion:
Understanding national efforts to extend voting rights

Ask students to read the first half of the section "Gaining the right to vote for black men," through the discussion of poll taxes. Indicate the need for all three Civil War Amendments:

- Because the South's defeat did not free the slaves, the Thirteenth Amendment was adopted.

- Because Southern states would not grant citizenship to blacks, the Fourteenth Amendment was adopted.

- Because Southern states said voting was not a right of United States citizenship, the Fifteenth Amendment was added.

Point out to the students the distinction between a constitutional amendment that establishes a right or freedom that cannot be taken away, and a congressional law that establishes methods of enforcing that right. Go over with the students the methods states used to attempt to get around the Fifteenth Amendment.

D. Reading and Discussion:
Understanding efforts to gain the right to vote

Form groups of three students each. Assign one student in each group to read the rest of the section "Gaining the right to vote for black men." Assign the second student in each group to read the section "Women gain the right to vote." The third student should read the remaining sections on Native Americans and eighteen-year-olds. Each student should read his or her assigned text section or sections and prepare a brief report for the other members in the group, using the form "Handout 20-1."

When group members have completed their reports, ask them to discuss within their groups the following question: Do you think our nation is more democratic today than it was in 1901? Why or why not? Call the class back together and poll them on the group responses to this question.

Assign the class the last section "Voting requirements today." Discuss with them the possible reasons for residency requirements as well as citizen requirements to vote in state elections.

Possible discussion questions could be:

- Should a student who entered your homeroom and school two days ago be allowed to vote for homeroom as well as school president? Why or why not?

- Should a student who is visiting from out-of-town and attending class be allowed to vote in your homeroom and school elections? Why or why not?

E. Concluding Activity

Conclude the lesson by leading a class discussion of the questions contained in "Reviewing and using the lesson." Allow time for students to work on their collages. By this time, they should be putting the collages together, so you may wish to supply the poster paper at this time.

OPTIONAL ACTIVITIES

For Reinforcement, Extended Learning, and Enrichment

1. You might ask students to play the role of a young black man who has just been denied the right to register to vote. They are to write a letter to a friend in the North and express their feelings. See Handout 20-2.

2. Interested students can find out your state's voting requirements and explain the rationale for them.

3. Have students find and list the amendments to the Constitution that protect citizens' right to vote. Make a timeline of these amendments. Identify the groups whose rights each amendment was written to protect.

4. Students could survey the number of adults who are registered to vote and who actually voted in the last general election. They might speculate on the reasons for low voter turnout.

Handout 20-1

Voting Rights Report

1. What group are you studying?_____

2. Describe any constitutional amendments that helped this group gain the right to vote.

3. Describe important events that happened or steps taken that helped this group gain the right to vote.

4. What dates or years are important to remember about the efforts of this group to gain the right to vote?

Handout 20-2

Letter to a Friend

It is 1893. You are a young black man living in the South. Today you went to register (sign up) to vote. But tonight you are still not a registered voter. Write a letter to a friend in a Northern state. Explain what happened to you today. (You can choose from any of the problems black voters faced.) Tell your friend how you feel about this experience. Do you think your constitutional rights were violated? What do you think should be done?

Unit Five

What are the responsibilities of citizens?

UNIT OVERVIEW

This concluding unit looks at issues raised by the question, "What are the responsibilities of citizens?" It emphasizes the relationship between rights and responsibilities. Specific responsibilities associated with the five basic rights discussed in Unit Four are examined.

The unit then discusses the citizen's responsibility to work for the common welfare, and examines the problem of deciding what the common welfare might be in situations involving conflicting interests.

Various forms of participation appropriate to the age group are discussed, including studying about government, becoming informed about current events, expressing opinions in discussions, writing letters to government officials, volunteering, and taking part in school government. Students are reminded that the type and level of participation they engage in is a personal decision they must make.

UNIT OBJECTIVES

At the conclusion of this unit:

1. Students should be able to identify responsibilities associated with certain basic rights of citizens and explain why they are important.

2. Students should be able to examine a problem concerning the common welfare, explain the responsibility of citizens to understand and attempt to solve the problem, and take and defend a position on a possible solution to the problem.

3. Students should be able to explain the importance of citizen participation.

4. Students should be able to describe various ways they may participate in their government.

UNIT INTRODUCTION

Tell students that the last unit deals with a question that concerns all of them, "What are the responsibilities of citizens?" Read the introduction to Unit Five aloud with the class. Emphasize that the unit will raise a number of important questions which each student must answer for himself or herself.

UNIT PROJECT (optional)

Have students look through newspapers or news magazines for evidence of individuals carrying out responsibilities as citizens. Based on their findings, compile a class list of ways to participate in our government. Post this list on the board and tell students that they can add to it as they learn more about participation.

Lesson 21

What responsibilities accompany our rights?

LESSON OVERVIEW

This lesson looks at an important question students will face as citizens: What responsibilities accompany our basic rights? The lesson begins with a class discussion of the importance of citizens fulfilling responsibilities in order to protect their rights. The class then engages in a problem-solving activity that examines specific responsibilities that might be connected with protecting the five basic rights studied in Unit Four, and poses the question of what might happen if citizens did not fulfill these responsibilities.

LESSON OBJECTIVES

At the conclusion of this lesson:

1. Students should be able to explain the importance of the fulfillment of responsibilities by citizens if everyone's rights are to be protected.

2. Students should be able to describe specific responsibilities associated with five essential rights of citizens.

MATERIALS NEEDED

Student text

TEACHING PROCEDURES

A. Introductory Activity:
Examining the importance of citizenship responsibilities

Have the students read the "Purpose of Lesson" and "Is a good constitution enough?" Go over the three prerequisites discussed in the text for the protection of rights: (1) a good constitution; (2) good leaders; and (3) good citizens.

B. Reading and Problem Solving:
Identifying a citizen's responsibilities

Have students read the first paragraph of the next section, "What responsibilities go along with our rights?" Then divide the class into five groups. Assign each group one set of questions in the problem-solving activity, "Can you have rights without responsibilities?" If the groups have more than five students, subdivide the groups so all students will have a chance to discuss the questions. Each group is to develop answers to its set of questions, write down the answers, and assign one or more members of the group to report the group's responses to the class. Allow time for class discussion of each group's responses. You may wish to develop a class consensus on what responsibilities should be associated with each of the basic rights discussed.

In a class discussion, have students consider these questions:

- Do most people understand these responsibilities and the importance of fulfilling them?

- How do young children learn these responsibilities?

- Would they add any other responsibilities to the list?

- Which responsibilities do they think are the most difficult to fulfill?

C. Concluding Activity

Conclude the lesson by leading a class discussion of the questions asked in "Reviewing and using the lesson."

OPTIONAL ACTIVITIES

For Reinforcement, Extended Learning, and Enrichment

1. Have students draw posters that illustrate responsibilities that are associated with each basic right.

2. Divide the class into groups of three to five students and have each group develop a skit that demonstrates a citizen's responsibility in a particular situation.

How can we promote the common welfare?

LESSON OVERVIEW

This lesson discusses the citizen's responsibility to promote the common welfare, and points out that sometimes it is not easy to decide what is in the common interest. It includes questions that may be asked about a situation in which there are conflicting interests, which might be helpful in reaching such a decision.

The lesson then considers the reasons for participating in government, and suggests ways in which students of this age group can participate. The lesson concludes by raising the question of a citizen's responsibility to help those in need of help, both in our own country and in other countries.

LESSON OBJECTIVES

At the conclusion of this lesson:

1. Students should be able to explain the responsibility of citizens to promote the common welfare, and the difficulties involved in deciding what the common welfare is in some situations.

2. Students should be able to give reasons for participating in government.

3. Students should be able to explain various ways they can participate in government before they are able to vote.

MATERIALS NEEDED

1. Student text

2. Handout 22-1

TEACHING PROCEDURES

A. Introductory Activity:
Determining our responsibility to the common welfare

Have students read the "Purpose of lesson" and "How do we decide what is best for everyone?" Review with the students the discussion in the problem-solving activity in Lesson 12, "How should Senator Smith vote?" Remind them of the difficulties elected legislators face in determining the common welfare. Possible discussion questions could be:

- How do legislators get information on what is best for everyone?

- How do they find out what the people they represent think is best?

- What are the responsibilities of good citizens to their elected legislators?

B. Problem Solving:
Deciding what is best for everyone

Divide the class into groups of three to five students. Ask each group to read through the problem-solving activity "What decision would you reach?" and answer the questions that follow it. Each group should then present its answers to the class. Allow time for class discussion of the various answers presented. You may wish to have the class vote on what is the best solution to the problem.

Possible discussion questions could be:

- What are the citizen's responsibilities after a decision has been made?

- What should citizens do if they feel the decision is not in the best interest of everyone?

- Are there any circumstances where a citizen is justified in peacefully disobeying a law to protest its unfairness?

C. Reading and Discussion:
Understanding the importance of participation

Have the students read the section, "How important is it for you to participate in your government?" Ask them to tell the ways they can participate that are discussed in the text. List the ways they can participate on the blackboard as they mention them. Ask if they can think of other ways they can participate before they become adults.

D. Reading and Discussion:
Deciding your own responsibilities

Have students read the last section, "What responsibilities will you fulfill?" Then have students complete Handout 22-1 as they consider possible ways they might participate in government as adults.

E. Concluding Activity

Conclude the lesson by leading a class discussion of the questions contained in "Reviewing and using the lesson."

OPTIONAL ACTIVITIES

For Reinforcement, Extended Learning, and Enrichment

1. Conduct a mock legislative hearing on the topic: Should citizens be required to vote? Divide the class into groups of four or five students for the class hearing. Allow time for the groups to discuss the bill that will be the subject of the hearing. You might assign roles to each student group: League of Women Voters, Democratic Party, Republican Party, Young Voters Association, Freedom Party, etc. You might wish to write a proposed law for the students to discuss.

2. Students can continue their search for articles and pictures depicting participation to see how many kinds of participation they can find.

3. Have students read the editorials and letters to the editor in the local newspaper to identify issues about which people in your community seem to be unhappy. Students could then design a citizen participation campaign to achieve the desired change or improvement.

Handout 22-1

Citizen Participation Checklist

DIRECTIONS: In the first column after each item below, place an I if you think the item is important. In the second column, place an X next to the items you would be likely to do:

Form of Participation	Important? (I)	Likely to Do? (X)
Signing up to vote in local, state, and national elections		
Voting in local, state, and national elections		
Trying to talk someone into voting a certain way		
Wearing a button or putting a sticker on your car		
Writing letters to elected representatives		
Giving money to a political candidate or cause you believe in		
Going to meetings to gain information, discuss issues, or lend support		
Handing out campaign literature or carrying a campaign sign		
Protesting against a law you feel is unjust		
Running for or holding public office		
Placing a campaign sign in your front window or front yard		
Helping to sign up other citizens to vote in upcoming elections		

Form of Participation	Important? (I)	Likely to Do (X)
Working in the office of a candidate or a cause that you support		
Keeping informed on the issues by reading and watching television		
Discussing the issues with friends and family		

Reference Section

Declaration of Independence

IN CONGRESS, JULY 4, 1776.

A DECLARATION

BY THE **REPRESENTATIVES** OF THE

UNITED STATES OF AMERICA,

IN GENERAL CONGRESS ASSEMBLED

WHEN in the Course of human Events, it becomes necessary for one People to dissolve the Political Bands which have connected them with another, and to assume among the Powers of the Earth, the separate and equal Station to which the Laws of Nature and of Nature's God entitle them, a decent Respect to the Opinions of Mankind requires that they should declare the causes which impel them to the Separation.

We hold these Truths to be self-evident, that all Men are created equal, that they are endowed by their Creator with certain unalienable Rights, that among these are Life, Liberty, and the Pursuit of Happiness--That to secure these Rights, Governments are instituted among Men, deriving their just Powers from the Consent of the Governed, that whenever any Form of Government becomes destructive of these Ends it is the Right of the People to alter or to abolish it, and to institute new Government, laying its Foundation on such Principles, and organizing its Powers in such Form, as to them shall seem most likely to effect their Safety and Happiness. Prudence, indeed, will dictate that Governments long established should not be changed for light and transient Causes; and accordingly all Experience hath shewn, that Mankind are more disposed to suffer, while Evils are sufferable, than to right themselves by abolishing the Forms to which they are accustomed. But when a long Train of Abuses and Usurpations, pursuing invariably the same Object, evinces a Design to reduce them under absolute Despotism, it is their Right, it is their Duty, to throw off such Government, and to provide new Guards for their future Security. Such has been the patient Sufferance of these Colonies; and such is now the Necessity which constrains them to alter their former Systems of Government. The History of the present King of Great-Britain is a History of repeated Injuries and Usurpations, all having in direct Object the Establishment of an absolute Tyranny over these States. To prove this, let Facts be submitted to a candid World.

He has refused his Assent to Laws, the most wholesome and necessary for the public Good.

He has forbidden his Governors to pass Laws of immediate and pressing Importance, unless suspended in their Operation till his Assent should be obtained; and when so suspended, he has utterly neglected to attend to them.

He has refused to pass other Laws for the Accommodation of large Districts of People, unless those People would relinquish the Right of Representation in the Legislature, a Right inestimable to them, and formidable to Tyrants only.

He has called together Legislative Bodies at Places unusual, uncomfortable, and distant from the Depository of their public Records, for the sole Purpose of fatiguing them into Compliance with his Measures.

He has dissolved Representative Houses repeatedly, for opposing with manly Firmness his Invasions on the Rights of the People.

He has refused for a long Time, after such Dissolutions, to cause others to be elected; whereby the Legislative Powers, incapable of Annihilation, have returned to the People at large for their exercise; the State remaining in the mean time exposed to all the Dangers of Invasions from without, and Convulsions within.

He has endeavored to prevent the Population of these States; for that Purpose obstructing the Laws for Naturalization of Foreigners; refusing to pass others to encourage their Migrations hither, and raising the Conditions of new Appropriations of Lands.

He has obstructed the Administration of Justice, by refusing his Assent to Laws for establishing Judiciary Powers.

He has made Judges dependent on his Will alone, for the Tenure of their Offices, and the Amount and Payment of their Salaries.

He has erected a Multitude of new Offices, and sent hither Swarms of Officers to harass our People and eat out their Substance.

He has kept among us, the Times of Peace, Standing Armies, without the consent of our Legislatures.

He has affected to render the Military independent of and superior to the Civil Power.

He has combined with others to subject us to a Jurisdiction foreign to our Constitution, and unacknowledged by our Laws; giving his Assent to their Acts of pretended Legislation:

For quartering large Bodies of Armed Troops among us:

For protecting them, by a mock Trial, from Punishment for any Murders which they should commit on the Inhabitants of these States:

For cutting off our Trade with all Parts of the World:

For imposing Taxes on us without our Consent:

For depriving us, in many Cases, of the Benefits of Trial by Jury:

For transporting us beyond Seas to be tried for pretended Offenses:

For abolishing the free System of English Laws in a neighbouring Province, establishing therein an Arbitrary Government, and enlarging its Boundaries, so as to render it at once an Example and fit Instrument for introducing the same absolute Rule into these Colonies:

For taking away our Charters, abolishing our most valuable Laws, and altering fundamentally the Forms of our Governments:

For suspending our own Legislatures, and declaring themselves invested with Power to legislate for us in all Cases whatsoever.

He has abdicated Government here, by declaring us out of his Protection and waging War against us.

He has plundered our Seas, ravaged our Coasts, burnt our Towns, and destroyed the Lives of our People.

He is, at this Time, transporting large Armies of foreign Mercenaries to compleat the Works of Death, Desolation, and Tyranny, already begun with circumstances of Cruelty and Perfidy, scarcely paralleled in the most barbarous Ages, and totally unworthy the Head of a civilized Nation.

He has constrained our fellow Citizens taken Captive on the high Seas to bear Arms against their Country, to become the Executioners of their Friends and Brethren, or to fall themselves by their Hands.

He has excited domestic Insurrections amongst us, and has endeavoured to bring on the Inhabitants of our Frontiers, the merciless Indian Savages, whose known Rule of Warfare, is an undistinguished Destruction, of all Ages, Sexes and Conditions.

In every stage of these Oppressions we have Petitioned for Redress in the most humble Terms: Our repeated Petitions have been answered only by repeated Injury. A Prince, whose Character is thus marked by every act which may define a Tyrant, is unfit to be the Ruler of a free People.

Nor have we been wanting in Attentions to our British Brethren. We have warned them from Time to Time of Attempts by their Legislature to extend an unwarrantable Jurisdiction over us. We have reminded them of the Circumstances of our Emigration and Settlement here. We have appealed to their native Justice and Magnanimity, and we have conjured them by the Ties of our common Kindred to disavow these Usurpations, which, would inevitably interrupt our Connections and Correspondence. They too have been deaf to the Voice of Justice and of Consanguinity. We must, therefore, acquiesce in the Necessity, which denounces our Separation, and hold them, as we hold the rest of Mankind, Enemies in War, in Peace, Friends.

We, therefore, the Representatives of the UNITED STATES OF AMERICA, in GENERAL CONGRESS, Assembled, appealing to the Supreme Judge of the World for the Rectitude of our Intentions, do, in the Name, and by Authority of the good People of these Colonies, solemnly Publish and Declare, That these United Colonies are, and of Right ought to be, FREE AND INDEPENDENT STATES; that they are absolved from all Allegiance to the British Crown, and that all political Connection between them and the State of Great-Britain, is and ought to be totally dissolved; and that as FREE AND INDEPENDENT STATES, they have full Power to levy War, conclude Peace, contract Alliances, establish Commerce, and to do all other Acts and Things which INDEPENDENT STATES may of right do. And for the support of this Declaration, with a firm Reliance on the Protection of divine Providence, we mutually pledge to each other our Lives, our Fortunes, and our sacred Honor.

Signed by ORDER and in BEHALF of the CONGRESS,
JOHN HANCOCK, PRESIDENT.

Signers of the Declaration of Independence

New-Hampshire
Josiah Bartlett,
Wm. Whipple,
Matthew Thornton.

Massachusetts-Bay
Saml. Adams,
John Adams,
Robt. Treat Paine,
Elbridge Gerry.

Rhode-Island and Providence, &c.
Step. Hopkins,
William Ellery.

Connecticut
Roger Sherman,
Saml. Huntington,
Wm. Williams,
Oliver Wolcott.

New-York
Wm. Floyd,
Phil. Livingston,
Frans. Lewis,
Lewis Morris.

New-Jersey
Richd. Stockton,
Jno. Witherspoon,
Fras. Hopkinson,
John Hart,
Abra. Clark.

Pennsylvania
Robt. Morris,
Benjamin Rush,
Benja. Franklin,
John Morton,
Geo. Clymer,
Jas. Smith,
Geo. Taylor,
James Wilson,
Geo. Ross.

Delaware
Casar Rodney,
Geo. Read,
(Tho M:Kean.)

Maryland
Samuel Chase,
Wm. Paca,
Thos. Stone,
Charles Carroll, of Carrollton.

Virginia
George Wythe,
Richard Henry Lee,
Ths. Jefferson,
Benja. Harrison,
Thos. Nelson, Jr.
Francis Lightfoot Lee,
Carter Braxton.

North-Carolina
Wm. Hooper,
Joseph Hewes,
John Penn.

South-Carolina
Edward Rutledge,
Thos. Heyward, Junr.
Thomas Lynch, Junr.
Arthur Middleton.

Georgia
Button Gwinnett,
Lyman Hall,
Geo. Walton.

According to the authenticated list printed by order of Congress of January 18, 1777.
Spelling, and abbreviations of names conform to original printed list.

The Constitution of the United States of America

Preamble

We the People of the United States, in Order to form a more perfect Union, establish Justice, insure domestic tranquility, provide for the common defence, promote the general Welfare, and secure the Blessings of Liberty to ourselves and our Posterity, do ordain and establish this Constitution for the United States of America.

ARTICLE I.

The Legislative Branch

Section 1.

All legislative Powers herein granted shall be vested in a Congress of the United States, which shall consist of a Senate and House of Representatives.

Section 2.

House of Representatives: Organization and Power of Impeachment

1. The House of Representatives shall be composed of Members chosen every second Year by the People of the several States, and the Electors in each State shall have the Qualifications requisite for Electors of the most numerous Branch of the State Legislature.

2. No Person shall be a Representative who shall not have attained to the Age of twenty five Years, and been seven Years a Citizen of the United States, and who shall not, when elected, be an Inhabitant of that State in which he shall be chosen.

3. [Representatives and direct Taxes shall be apportioned among the several States which may be included within this Union, according to their respective Numbers, which shall be determined by adding to the whole Number of free Persons, including those bound to Service for a Term of Years, and excluding Indians not taxed, three fifths of all other Persons.]* The actual Enumeration shall be made within three Years after the first Meeting of the Congress of the United States, and within every subsequent Term of ten Years, in such Manner as they shall by Law direct. The number of Representatives shall not

exceed one for every thirty Thousand, but each State shall have at Least one Representative; and until such enumeration shall be made, the State of New Hampshire shall be entitled to choose three, Massachusetts eight, Rhode Island and Providence Plantations one, Connecticut five, New York six, New Jersey four, Pennsylvania eight, Delaware one, Maryland six, Virginia ten, North Carolina five, South Carolina five, and Georgia three.

4. When vacancies happen in the Representation from any State, the Executive Authority thereof shall issue Writs of Election to fill such Vacancies.

5. The House of Representatives shall choose their Speaker and other Officers; and shall have the sole Power of Impeachment.

Section 3.

The Senate, Organization and Powers of Impeachment

1. The Senate of the United States shall be composed of two Senators from each State, [chosen by the Legislature thereof,]** for six Years; and each Senator shall have one Vote.

2. Immediately after they shall be assembled in Consequence of the first Election, they shall be divided as equally as may be into three Classes. The seats of the Senators of the first Class shall be vacated at the Expiration of the second Year, of the second Class at the Expiration of the fourth Year, and of the third Class at the Expiration of the sixth Year, so that one third may be chosen every second Year; [and if Vacancies happen by Resignation, or otherwise, during the Recess of the Legislature of any State, the Executive thereof may make temporary Appointments until the next Meeting of the Legislature, which shall then fill such Vacancies.]**

3. No Person shall be a Senator who shall not have attained to the Age of thirty Years, and been nine Years a Citizen of the United States, and who shall not, when elected, be an Inhabitant of that State for which he shall be chosen.

*   Changed by section 2 of the Fourteenth Amendment.
**   Changed by the Seventeenth Amendment.

4. The Vice President of the United States shall be President of the Senate, but shall have no Vote, unless they be equally divided.

5. The Senate shall choose their other officers, and also a President pro tempore, in the Absence of the Vice President, or when he shall exercise the Office of President of the United States.

6. The Senate shall have the sole Power to try all Impeachments. When sitting for that Purpose, they shall be on Oath or Affirmation. When the President of the United States is tried, the Chief Justice shall preside: And no person shall be convicted without the Concurrence of two thirds of the Members present.

7. Judgment in Cases of Impeachment shall not extend further than to removal from Office, and disqualification to hold and enjoy any Office of honor, Trust or Profit under the United States; but the Party convicted shall nevertheless be liable and subject to Indictment, Trial, Judgment and Punishment, according to Law.

Section 4.
Elections and Meeting of Congress

1. The Times, Places and Manner of holding Elections for Senators and Representatives shall be prescribed in each State by the Legislature thereof; but the Congress may at any time by Law make or alter such Regulations, except as to the Places of choosing Senators.

2. The Congress shall assemble at least once in every Year, and such Meeting shall be [on the first Monday in December,]* unless they shall by Law appoint a different Day.

Section 5.
Congress's Rules of Procedure, Powers, Quorum, Journals, Meetings, Adjournments

1. Each House shall be the Judge of the Elections, Returns and Qualifications of its own Members, and a Majority of each shall constitute a Quorum to do Business; but a smaller Number may adjourn from day to day, and may be authorized to compel the Attendance of absent Members, in such Manner, and under such Penalties as each House may provide.

2. Each House may determine the Rules of its Proceedings, punish its members for disorder-

ly Behavior, and, with the Concurrence of two thirds, expel a Member.

3. Each House shall keep a Journal of its Proceedings, and from time to time publish the same, excepting such Parts as may in their Judgment require Secrecy; and the Yeas and Nays of the Members of either House on any question shall, at the Desire of one fifth of those Present, be entered on the Journal.

4. Neither House, during the Session of Congress, shall, without the Consent of the other, adjourn for more than three days, nor to any other Place than that in which the two Houses shall be sitting.

Section 6.
Pay, Privileges, Limitations

1. The Senators and Representatives shall receive a Compensation for their Services, to be ascertained by Law, and paid out of the Treasury of the United States. They shall in all cases, except Treason, Felony and Breach of the Peace, be privileged from Arrest during their Attendance at the Session of their respective Houses, and in going to and returning from the same; and for any Speech or Debate in either House, they shall not be questioned in any other Place.

2. No Senator or Representative shall, during the Time for which he was elected, be appointed to any civil Office under the Authority of the United States, which shall have been created, or the Emoluments whereof shall have been increased during such time; and no Person holding any Office under the United States, shall be a Member of either House during his Continuance in Office.

Section 7.
Procedure in Passing Bills, President's Veto Power

1. All Bills for raising Revenue shall originate in the House of Representatives; but the Senate may propose or concur with Amendments as on other Bills.

2. Every Bill which shall have passed the House of Representatives and the Senate, shall, before it becomes a Law, be presented to the President of the United States; if he approve he shall sign it, but if not he shall return it, with his Objections, to that House in which it shall have originated, who shall enter the Objections at large on their Journal, and proceed to reconsider

---

* Changed by section 2 of the Twentieth Amendment.

it. If after such Reconsideration two thirds of that House shall agree to pass the Bill, it shall be sent, together with the Objections, to the other House, by which it shall likewise be reconsidered, and if approved by two thirds of that House, it shall become a Law. But in all such Cases the Votes of both Houses shall be determined by yeas and nays, and the Names of the Persons voting for and against the Bill shall be entered on the Journal of each House respectively. If any Bill shall not be returned by the President within ten Days (Sundays excepted) after it shall have been presented to him, the Same shall be a Law, in like Manner as if he had signed it, unless the Congress by their Adjournment prevent its Return, in which Case it shall not be a Law.

3. Every Order, Resolution, or Vote to which the Concurrence of the Senate and House of Representatives may be necessary (except on a question of Adjournment) shall be presented to the President of the United States; and before the Same shall take Effect, shall be approved by him, or being disapproved by him, shall be repassed by two thirds of the Senate and House of Representatives, according to the Rules and Limitations prescribed in the Case of a Bill.

Section 8.
Powers Delegated to Congress
The Congress shall have Power

1. To lay and collect Taxes, Duties, Imposts and Excises, to pay the Debts and provide for the common Defence and general Welfare of the United States; but all Duties, Imposts and Excises shall be uniform throughout the United States;

2. To borrow Money on the credit of the United States;

3. To regulate Commerce with foreign Nations, and among the several States, and with the Indian Tribes;

4. To establish an uniform Rule of Naturalization, and uniform Laws on the subject of Bankruptcies throughout the United States;

5. To coin Money, regulate the Value thereof, and of Foreign Coin, and fix the Standard of Weights and Measures;

6. To provide for the Punishment of counterfeiting the Securities and current Coin of the United States;

7. To establish Post Offices and post Roads;

8. To promote the Progress of Science and useful Arts, by securing for limited Times to Authors and Inventors the exclusive Right to their respective Writings and Discoveries;

9. To constitute Tribunals inferior to the supreme Court;

10. To define and punish Piracies and Felonies committed on the high Seas, and Offenses against the Law of Nations;

11. To declare War, grant Letters of Marque and Reprisal, and make Rules concerning Captures on Land and Water;

12. To raise and support Armies, but no Appropriation of Money to that Use shall be for a longer Term than two Years;

13. To provide and maintain a Navy;

14. To make Rules for the Government and Regulation of the land and naval Forces;

15. To provide for calling forth the Militia to execute the Laws of the Union, suppress Insurrections and repel Invasions;

16. To provide for organizing, arming, and disciplining the Militia, and for governing such Part of them as may be employed in the Service of the United States, reserving to the States respectively, the Appointment of the Officers, and the Authority of training the Militia according to the discipline prescribed by Congress;

17. To exercise exclusive Legislation in all Cases whatsoever, over such District (not exceeding ten Miles square) as may, by Cession of particular States, and the Acceptance of Congress, become the Seat of the Government of the United States, and to exercise like Authority over all Places purchased by the Consent of the Legislature of the State in which the Same shall be, for the Erection of Forts, Magazines, Arsenals, dock-Yards and other needful Buildings; — And

18. To make all Laws which shall be necessary and proper for carrying into Execution the foregoing powers, and all other Powers vested by this Constitution in the Government of the United States, or in any Department or Officer thereof.

Section 9.
Powers Denied to Congress

1. The Migration or Importation of such Persons as any of the States now existing shall think proper to admit, shall not be prohibited by the Congress prior to the Year one thousand eight hundred and eight, but a Tax or duty may be imposed on such Importation, not exceeding ten dollars for each Person.

2. The Privilege of the Writ of Habeas Corpus shall not be suspended, unless when in Cases of Rebellion or Invasion the public Safety may require it.

3. No Bill of Attainder or ex post facto Law shall be passed.

4. [No Capitation, or other direct, Tax shall be laid, unless in Proportion to the Census or Enumeration herein before directed to be taken.]*

5. No Tax or Duty shall be laid on Articles exported from any State.

6. No Preference shall be given by any Regulation of Commerce or Revenue to the Ports of one State over those of another: nor shall Vessels bound to, or from, one State, be obliged to enter, clear, or pay Duties in another.

7. No Money shall be drawn from the Treasury, but in Consequence of Appropriations made by Law; and a regular Statement and Account of the Receipts and Expenditures of all public Money shall be published from time to time.

8. No Title of Nobility shall be granted by the United States: And no Person holding any Office of Profit or Trust under them, shall, without the Consent of the Congress, accept of any present, Emolument, Office, or Title, of any kind whatever, from any King, Prince, or foreign State.

Section 10.
Restrictions on States' Powers

1. No State shall enter into any Treaty, Alliance, or Confederation; grant Letters of Marque and Reprisal; coin Money; emit Bills of Credit; make any Thing but gold and silver Coin a Tender in Payment of Debts; pass any Bill of Attainder, ex post facto Law, or Law impairing the Obligation of Contracts, or grant any Title of Nobility.

* Changed by the Sixteenth Amendment.

2. No State shall, without the Consent of the Congress, lay any Imposts or Duties on Imports or Exports, except what may be absolutely necessary for executing its inspection Laws: and the net Produce of all Duties and Imposts, laid by any State on Imports or Exports, shall be for the Use of the Treasury of the United States; and all such Laws shall be subject to the Revision and Control of the Congress.

3. No State shall, without the Consent of Congress, lay any Duty of Tonnage, keep Troops, or Ships of War in time of Peace, enter into any Agreement or Compact with another State, or with a foreign Power, or engage in War, unless actually invaded, or in such imminent Danger as will not admit of delay.

ARTICLE II.

The Executive Branch
Section 1.
President and Vice-President: Election, Qualifications, and Oath

1. The executive Power shall be vested in a President of the United States of America. He shall hold his Office during the term of four Years, and, together with the Vice President, chosen for the same Term, be elected, as follows.

2. Each State shall appoint, in such Manner as the Legislature thereof may direct, a Number of Electors, equal to the whole Number of Senators and Representatives to which the State may be entitled in the Congress: but no Senator or Representative, or Person holding an Office of Trust or Profit under the United States, shall be appointed an Elector.

3. [The Electors shall meet in their respective states, and vote by Ballot for two Persons, of whom one at least shall not be an Inhabitant of the same State with themselves. And they shall make a List of all the Persons voted for, and of the Number of Votes for each; which List they shall sign and certify, and transmit sealed to the Seat of the Government of the United States, directed to the President of the Senate. The President of the Senate shall, in the Presence of the Senate and House of Representatives, open all the Certificates, and the Votes shall then be counted. The Person having the greatest Number of Votes shall be the President, if such Number be a Majority of the whole Number of Electors appointed; and if there be more than one who have such Majority, and have an equal Number of Votes, then the House of Representatives shall immediately choose by Ballot one of them for President; and if no Person have a Majority, then from the five highest on the List the said House shall in like manner choose the President. But in choosing the President, the Votes shall be taken by States, the Representation from each State having one Vote; A quorum for this Purpose shall consist of a Member or Members from two thirds of the States, and a Majority of all the States shall be necessary to a Choice. In every Case, after the Choice of the President, the Person having the greatest Number of Votes of the Electors shall be the Vice President. But if there should remain two or more who have equal Votes, the Senate shall choose from them by Ballot the Vice President.]*

4. The Congress may determine the Time of choosing the Electors, and the day on which they shall give their Votes; which Day shall be the same throughout the United States.

5. No Person except a natural born Citizen, or a Citizen of the United States at the time of the Adoption of this Constitution, shall be eligible to the Office of the President; neither shall any person be eligible to that Office who shall not have attained to the Age of thirty five Years, and been fourteen Years a Resident within the United States.

6. [In Case of the Removal of the President from Office, or of his Death, Resignation, or Inability to discharge the Powers and Duties of the said Office, the Same shall devolve on the Vice President, and the Congress may by Law provide for the Case of Removal, Death, Resignation or Inability, both of the President and Vice President, declaring what Officer shall then act as President, and such Officer shall act accordingly, until the Disability be removed, or a President shall be elected.]**

7. The President shall, at stated Times, receive for his Services, a Compensation, which shall neither be increased nor diminished during the Period for which he shall have been elected, and he shall not receive within that Period any other Emolument from the United States, or any of them.

8. Before he enter the Execution of his Office, he shall take the following Oath or Affirma-

tion: — "I do solemnly swear (or affirm) that I will faithfully execute the Office of President of the United States, and will to the best of my Ability, preserve, protect, and defend the Constitution of the United States."

Section 2.
Powers of the President

1. The President shall be Commander in Chief of the Army and Navy of the United States, and of the Militia of the several States, when called into the actual Service of the United States; he may require the Opinion, in writing, of the principal Officer in each of the executive Departments, upon any Subject relating to the Duties of their respective Offices, and he shall have Power to grant Reprieves and Pardons for Offenses against the United States, except in Cases of Impeachment.

2. He shall have Power, by and with the Advice and Consent of the Senate, to make Treaties, provided two thirds of the Senators present concur; and he shall nominate, and by and with the Advice and Consent of the Senate, shall appoint Ambassadors, other public Ministers and Consuls, Judges of the supreme Court, and all other Officers of the United States, whose Appointments are not herein otherwise provided for, and which shall be established by Law: but the Congress may by Law vest the Appointment of such inferior Officers, as they think proper, in the President alone, in the Courts of Law, or in the Heads of Departments.

3. The President shall have Power to fill up all Vacancies that may happen during the Recess of the Senate, by granting Commissions which shall expire at the End of their next Session.

Section 3.
Duties of the President

He shall from time to time give to the Congress Information of the State of the Union, and recommend to their Consideration such Measures as he shall judge necessary and expedient; he may, on extraordinary Occasions, convene both Houses, or either of them, and in Case of Disagreement between them, with Respect to the Time of Adjournment, he may adjourn them to such Time as he shall think proper; he shall receive Ambassadors and other public Ministers; he shall take Care that the Laws be

* Changed by the Twelfth Amendment.
** Changed by the Twenty-Fifth Amendment.

faithfully executed, and shall Commission all the Officers of the United States.

Section 4.
Impeachment and Removal from Office for Crimes

The President, Vice President and all civil Officers of the United States, shall be removed from Office on Impeachment for, and Conviction of, Treason, Bribery, or other high Crimes and Misdemeanors.

ARTICLE III.
The Judicial Branch
Section 1.
Federal Courts, Tenure of Office

The judicial Power of the United States, shall be vested in one supreme Court, and in such inferior Courts as the Congress may from time to time ordain and establish. The Judges, both of the supreme and inferior Courts, shall hold their Offices during good Behavior, and shall, at stated Times, receive for their Services a Compensation, which shall not be diminished during their Continuance in Office.

Section 2.
Jurisdiction of Federal Courts

1. The judicial Power shall extend to all Cases, in Law and Equity, arising under this Constitution, the Laws of the United States, and Treaties made, or which shall be made, under their Authority;— to all Cases affecting Ambassadors, other public Ministers and Consuls;— to all Cases of admiralty and maritime Jurisdiction;— to Controversies to which the United States shall be a Party;— to Controversies between two or more States; [between a State and Citizens of another State;]* between Citizens of different States;—between Citizens of the same State claiming Lands under Grants of different States;—[and between a State, or the Citizens thereof, and foreign States, Citizens or Subjects.]*

2. In all Cases affecting Ambassadors, other public Ministers and Consuls, and those in which a State shall be Party, the supreme Court shall have original Jurisdiction. In all the other Cases before mentioned, the supreme Court shall have appellate Jurisdiction, both as to Law and Fact,

with such Exceptions, and under such Regulations as the Congress shall make.

3. The Trial of all Crimes, except in Cases of Impeachment, shall be by Jury; and such Trial shall be held in the State where said Crimes shall have been committed; but when not committed within any State, the Trial shall be at such Place or Places as the Congress may by Law have directed.

Section 3.
Treason: Conviction Of and Punishment For

1. Treason against the United States shall consist only in levying War against them, or in adhering to their Enemies, giving them Aid and Comfort. No Person shall be convicted of Treason unless on the Testimony of two Witnesses to the same overt Act, or on Confession in open Court.

2. The Congress shall have Power to declare the Punishment of Treason, but no Attainder of Treason shall work Corruption of Blood, or Forfeiture except during the Life of the Person attainted.

ARTICLE IV.
Relations Among the States
Section 1.
Full Faith and Credit

Full Faith and Credit shall be given in each State to the public Acts, Records, and judicial Proceedings of every other State; And the Congress may by general Laws prescribe the manner in which such Acts, Records and Proceedings shall be proved, and the Effect thereof.

Section 2.
Rights of State Citizens; Right of Extradition

1. The Citizens of each State shall be entitled to all Privileges and Immunities of Citizens in the several States.

2. A Person charged in any State with Treason, Felony, or other Crime, who shall flee from Justice, and be found in another State, shall on Demand of the executive Authority of the State from which he fled, be delivered up, to be removed to the State having Jurisdiction of the Crime.

* Changed by the Eleventh Amendment.

3. [No person held to Service or Labour in one State, under the Laws thereof, escaping into another, shall, in Consequence of any Law or Regulation therein, be discharged from such Service or Labour, but shall be delivered up on Claim of the Party to whom such Service or Labour may be due.]*

Section 3.
Admission of New States

1. New States may be admitted by the Congress into this Union; but no new State shall be formed or erected within the Jurisdiction of any other State; nor any State be formed by the Junction of two or more States, or parts of States, without the Consent of the Legislatures of the States concerned as well as of the Congress.

2. The Congress shall have Power to dispose of and make all needful Rules and Regulations respecting the territory or other Property belonging to the United States; and nothing in this Constitution shall be so construed as to Prejudice any Claims of the United States, or of any particular State.

Section 4.
Republican Government Guaranteed

The United States shall guarantee to every State in this Union a Republican Form of Government, and shall protect each of them against Invasion; and on Application of the Legislature, or of the Executive (when the Legislature cannot be convened) against domestic Violence.

ARTICLE V.
Amendment Procedures

The Congress, whenever two thirds of both Houses shall deem it necessary, shall propose Amendments to this Constitution, or, on the Application of the Legislatures of two thirds of the several States, shall call a Convention for proposing Amendments, which, in either Case, shall be valid to all Intents and Purposes, as Part of this Constitution, when ratified by the Legislatures of three fourths of the several States, or by Conventions in three fourths thereof, as the one or the other Mode of Ratification may be proposed by the Congress; Provided that no Amendment which may be made prior to the Year One thousand eight hundred and eight shall in any Manner affect the first and fourth Clauses in the Ninth Section of the first Article; and that no

* Changed by the Thirteenth Amendment.

State, without its Consent, shall be deprived of its equal Suffrage in the Senate.

ARTICLE VI.
Supremacy of the Constitution and Federal Laws

1. All debts contracted and Engagements entered into, before the Adoption of this Constitution, shall be as valid against the United States under this Constitution, as under the Confederation.

2. This Constitution, and the Laws of the United States which shall be made in Pursuance thereof; and all Treaties made, or which shall be made, under the Authority of the United States, shall be the supreme Law of the Land; and the Judges in every State shall be bound thereby, any Thing in the Constitution or Laws of any State to the Contrary notwithstanding.

3. The Senators and Representatives before mentioned, and the Members of the several State Legislatures, and all executive and judicial Officers, both of the United States and of the several States, shall be bound by Oath or Affirmation, to support this Constitution; but no religious Test shall ever be required as a Qualification to any Office or public Trust under the United States.

ARTICLE VII.
Ratification

The Ratification of the Conventions of nine States, shall be sufficient for the Establishment of this Constitution between the States so ratifying the Same.

Done in Convention by the unanimous consent of the States present the seventeenth day of September in the year of our Lord one thousand seven hundred and eighty seven and of the Independence of the United States of America the Twelfth. In witness whereof we have hereunto subscribed our Names,

George Washington — President
and deputy from Virginia

This constitution was adopted on September 17, 1787 by the Constitutional Convention, and was declared ratified on July 2, 1788.

Signers of the Constitution

New Hampshire

John Langdon

Nicholas Gilman

Massachusetts

Nathaniel Gorham

Rufus King

Connecticut

William Samuel Johnson

Roger Sherman

New York

Alexander Hamilton

New Jersey

William Livingston

David Brearley

William Paterson

Jonathan Dayton

Pennsylvania

Benjamin Franklin

Thomas Mifflin

Robert Morris

George Clymer

Thomas Fitzsimons

Jared Ingersoll

James Wilson

Gouverneur Morris

Delaware

George Read

Gunning Bedford, Jr.

John Dickinson

Richard Bassett

Jacob Broom

Maryland

James McHenry

Daniel of St. Tho. Jenifer

Daniel Carrol

Virginia

John Blair

James Madison, Jr.

North Carolina

William Blount

Richard Dobbs Spaight

Hugh Williamson

South Carolina

John Rutledge

Charles Cotesworth Pinckney

Charles Pinckney

Pierce Butler

Georgia

William Few

Abraham Baldwin

Attest *William Jackson*
Secretary

Amendments to the Constitution

Since 1787, twenty-six amendments have been proposed by the Congress and ratified by the several states, pursuant to the fifth Article of the original Constitution.

Amendment I.

Freedom of Religion and Expression

Congress shall make no law respecting an establishment of religion, or prohibiting the free exercise thereof; or abridging the freedom of speech, or of the press, or the right of the people peaceably to assemble, and to petition the Government for a redress of grievances. (Ratified December, 1791.)

Amendment II.

Right to Bear Arms

A well regulated Militia, being necessary to the security of a free State, the right of the people to keep and bear Arms, shall not be infringed. (Ratified December, 1791.)

Amendment III.

Quartering of Soldiers

No Soldier shall, in time of peace be quartered in any house, without the consent of the Owner, nor in time of war, but in a manner to be prescribed by law. (Ratified December, 1791.)

Amendment IV.

Security From Unreasonable Searches and Seizures

The right of the people to be secure in their persons, houses, papers, and effects, against unreasonable searches and seizures, shall not be violated, and no Warrants shall issue, but upon probable cause, supported by Oath or affirmation, and particularly describing the place to be searched, and the persons or things to be seized. (Ratified December, 1791.)

Amendment V.

Rights of Due Process of Law

No person shall be held to answer for a capital, or otherwise infamous crime, unless on a presentment or indictment of a Grand Jury, except in cases arising in the land or naval forces, or in the Militia, when in actual service in time of War or public danger; nor shall any person be subject for the same offence to be twice put in jeopardy of life or limb, nor shall be compelled in any criminal case to be a witness against himself, nor be deprived of life, liberty, or property, without due process of law; nor shall private property be taken for public use without just compensation. (Ratified December, 1791.)

Amendment VI.

Right to a Fair Trial

In all criminal prosecutions, the accused shall enjoy the right to a speedy and public trial, by an impartial jury of the State and district wherein the crime shall have been committed; which district shall have been previously ascertained by law, and to be informed of the nature and cause of the accusation; to be confronted with the witnesses against him; to have compulsory process for obtaining witnesses in his favor, and to have the assistance of counsel for his defence. (Ratified December, 1791.)

Amendment VII.

Trial by Jury

In Suits at common law, where the value in controversy shall exceed twenty dollars, the right of trial by jury shall be preserved, and no fact tried by a jury shall be otherwise re-examined in any Court of the United States, than according to the rules of the common law. (Ratified December, 1791.)

Amendment VIII.

Fair Bail and Punishments

Excessive bail shall not be required, nor excessive fines imposed, nor cruel and unusual punishments inflicted. (Ratified December, 1791.)

Amendment IX.

Rights Retained by the People

The enumeration in the Constitution of certain rights shall not be construed to deny or disparage others retained by the people. (Ratified December, 1791.)

Amendment X.

Powers Reserved to States and People

The powers not delegated to the United States by the Constitution, nor prohibited by it to the States, are reserved to the States respectively, or to the people. (Ratified December, 1791.)

Amendment XI.

Limitations on Federal Courts

The Judicial power of the United States shall not be construed to extend to any suit in law or equity, commenced or prosecuted against one of the United States by Citizens of another State, or by Citizens or Subjects of any Foreign State. (Ratified February, 1795.)

Amendment XII.

Election of President

The Electors shall meet in their respective states, and vote by ballot for President and Vice President, one of whom, at least, shall not be an inhabitant of the same state with themselves; they shall name in their ballots the person voted for as President, and in distinct ballots the person voted for as Vice-President, and they shall make distinct lists of all persons voted for as President, and of all persons voted for as Vice-President, and of the number of votes for each, which lists they shall sign and certify, and transmit sealed to the seat of the government of the United States, directed to the President of the Senate;—The President of the Senate shall, in the presence of the Senate and House of Representatives, open all the certificates and the votes shall then be counted;—The person having the greatest number of votes for President, shall be the President, if such number be a majority of the whole number of Electors appointed; and if no person have such majority, then from the persons having the highest numbers not exceeding three on the list of those voted for as President, the House of Representatives shall choose immediately, by ballot, the President. But in choosing the President, the votes shall be taken by states, the representation from each state having one vote; a quorum for this purpose shall consist of a member or members from two-thirds of the states, and a majority of all the states shall be necessary to a choice. [And if the House of Representatives shall not choose a President whenever the right of choice shall devolve upon them, before the fourth day of March next following, then the Vice-President shall act as President, as in the case of the death or other constitutional disability of the President—]* The person having the greatest number of votes as Vice-President, shall be the Vice-President, if such number be a majority of the whole number of Electors appointed, and if no person have a majority, then from the two highest numbers on the list, the Senate shall choose the Vice-President; a quorum for the purpose shall consist of two-thirds of the whole number of Senators, and a majority of the whole number shall be necessary to a choice. But no person constitutionally ineligible to the office of President shall be eligible to that of Vice-President of the United States. (Ratified June, 1804.)

Amendment XIII.

Slavery Abolished

Section 1. Neither slavery nor involuntary servitude, except as a punishment for crime whereof the party shall have been duly convicted, shall exist within the United States, or any place subject to their jurisdiction.

Section 2. Congress shall have power to enforce this article by appropriate legislation. (Ratified December, 1865.)

Amendment XIV.

Equal Protection and Due Process; Citizenship Defined and Guaranteed

Section 1. All persons born or naturalized in the United States and subject to the jurisdiction thereof, are citizens of the United States and of the State wherein they reside. No State shall make or enforce any law which shall abridge the privileges or immunities of citizens of the United States; nor shall any State deprive any person of life, liberty, or property, without due process of law; nor deny to any person within its jurisdiction the equal protection of the laws.

Section 2. Representatives shall be apportioned among the several States according to their respective numbers, counting the whole number of persons in each State, excluding Indians not taxed. But when the right to vote at any election for the choice of electors for President and Vice President of the United States, Representatives in Congress, the Executive and Judicial officers of a State, or the members of the Legislature thereof, is denied to any of the male inhabitants of such State, being twenty-one years of age, and citizens of the United States, or in any way abridged, except for participation in rebellion, or other crime, the basis of representation therein shall be reduced in the proportion which the number of such male citizens shall bear to the whole number of male citizens twenty-one years of age in such State.

---

*   Superseded by section 3 of the Twentieth Amendment.

Section 3. No person shall be a Senator or a Representative in Congress, or elector of President and Vice President, or hold any office, civil or military, under the United States, or under any State, who, having previously taken an oath, as a member of Congress, or as an officer of the United States, or as a member of any State legislature, or as an executive or judicial officer of any State, to support the Constitution of the United States, shall have engaged in insurrection or rebellion against the same, or given aid or comfort to the enemies thereof. But Congress may by a vote of two-thirds of each House, remove such disability.

Section 4. The validity of the public debt of the United States, authorized by law, including debts incurred for payment of pensions and bounties for services in suppressing insurrection or rebellion, shall not be questioned. But neither the United States nor any State shall assume or pay any debt or obligation incurred in aid of insurrection or rebellion against the United States, or any claim for the loss or emancipation of any slave; but all such debts, obligations and claims shall be held illegal and void.

Section 5. The Congress shall have power to enforce, by appropriate legislation, the provisions of this article. (Ratified July, 1868.)

Amendment XV.

Blacks' Right to Vote

Section 1. The right of citizens of the United States to vote shall not be denied or abridged by the United States or by any State on account of race, color, or previous condition of servitude.

Section 2. The Congress shall have power to enforce this article by appropriate legislation. (Ratified February, 1870.)

Amendment XVI.

Power to Tax Incomes

The Congress shall have power to lay and collect taxes on incomes, from whatever source derived, without apportionment among the several States, and without regard to any census or enumeration. (Ratified February, 1913.)

Amendment XVII.

Popular Election of Senators

The Senate of the United States shall be composed of two Senators from each State, elected by the people thereof, for six years; and

* Repealed by the Twenty-First Amendment.

each Senator shall have one vote. The electors in each State shall have the qualifications requisite for electors of the most numerous branch of the State legislatures.

When vacancies happen in the representation of any State in the Senate, the executive authority of such State shall issue writs of election to fill such vacancies: Provided, That the legislature of any State may empower the executive thereof to make temporary appointments until the people fill the vacancies by election as the legislature may direct.

This amendment shall not be so construed as to affect the election or term of any Senator chosen before it becomes valid as part of the Constitution. (Ratified April, 1913.)

Amendment XVIII.

Prohibition of Alcoholic Beverages

[Section 1. After one year from the ratification of this article the manufacture, sale, or transportation of intoxicating liquors within, the importation thereof into, or the exportation thereof from the United States and all territory subject to the jurisdiction thereof for beverage purposes is hereby prohibited.

Section 2. The Congress and the several States shall have concurrent power to enforce this article by appropriate legislation.

Section 3. This article shall be inoperative unless it shall have been ratified as an amendment to the Constitution by the legislatures of the several States, as provided in the Constitution, within seven years from the date of the submission hereof to the States by the Congress.]* (Ratified January, 1919.)

Amendment XIX.

Female Suffrage

The right of citizens of the United States to vote shall not be denied or abridged by the United States or by any State on account of sex.

Congress shall have power to enforce this article by appropriate legislation. (Ratified August, 1920.)

Amendment XX.

Changes in Terms of President and Congress

Section 1. The terms of the President and Vice President shall end at noon on the 20th day of January, and the terms of Senators and Representatives at noon on the 3d day of January, of the years in which such terms would have ended if this article had not been ratified; and the terms of their successors shall then begin.

Section 2. The Congress shall assemble at least once in every year, and such meeting shall begin at noon on the 3d day of January, unless they shall by law appoint a different day.

Section 3. If, at the time fixed for the beginning of the term of the President, the President elect shall have died, the Vice President elect shall become President. If a President shall not have been chosen before the time fixed for the beginning of his term, or if the President elect shall have failed to qualify, then the Vice President elect shall act as President until a President shall have qualified; and the Congress may by law provide for the case wherein neither a President elect nor a Vice President elect shall have qualified, declaring who shall then act as President, or the manner in which one who is to act shall be selected, and such person shall act accordingly until a President or Vice President shall have qualified.

Section 4. The Congress may by law provide for the case of the death of any of the persons from whom the House of Representatives may choose a President whenever the right of choice shall have devolved upon them, and for the case of the death of any of the persons from whom the Senate may choose a Vice President whenever the right of choice shall have devolved upon them.

Section 5. Sections 1 and 2 shall take effect on the 15th day of October following the ratification of this article.

Section 6. This article shall be inoperative unless it shall have been ratified as an amendment to the Constitution by the legislatures of three-fourths of the several States within seven years from the date of its submission. (Ratified January, 1933.)

Amendment XXI.

Repeal of Alcohol Prohibition

Section 1. The eighteenth article of amendment to the Constitution of the United States is hereby repealed.

Section 2. The transportation or importation into any State, Territory, or possession of the United States for delivery or use therein of intoxicating liquors, in violation of the laws thereof, is hereby prohibited.

Section 3. This article shall be inoperative unless it shall have been ratified as an amendment to the Constitution by conventions in the several States, as provided in the Constitution, within seven years from the date of the submission hereof to the States by the Congress. (Ratified December, 1933.)

Amendment XXII.

President Limited to Two Terms

Section 1. No person shall be elected to the office of the President more than twice, and no person who has held the office of President, or acted as President, for more than two years of a term to which some other person was elected President shall be elected to the office of the President more than once. But this Article shall not apply to any person holding the office of President when this Article was proposed by the Congress, and shall not prevent any person who may be holding the office of President, or acting as President, during the term within which this Article becomes operative from holding the office of President or acting as President during the remainder of such term.

Section 2. This article shall be inoperative unless it shall have been ratified as an amendment to the Constitution by the legislatures of three-fourths of the several States within seven years from the date of its submission to the States by the Congress. (Ratified February, 1951.)

Amendment XXIII.

Presidential Suffrage for District of Columbia

Section 1. The District constituting the seat of Government of the United States shall appoint in such manner as the Congress may direct:

A number of electors of President and Vice President equal to the whole number of Senators and Representatives in Congress to which the District would be entitled if it were a State, but in no event more than the least populous State; they shall be in addition to those appointed by the States, but they shall be considered, for the purposes of the election of President and Vice President, to be electors appointed by a State; and they shall meet in the District and perform such duties as provided by the twelfth article of amendment.

Section 2. The Congress shall have power to enforce this article by appropriate legislation. (Ratified March, 1961.)

Amendment XXIV.

Poll Tax Forbidden

Section 1. The right of citizens of the United States to vote in any primary or other election for President or Vice President, for electors for President or Vice President, or for Senator or Representative in Congress, shall not be denied or abridged by the United States or any State by reason of failure to pay any poll tax or other tax.

Section 2. The Congress shall have power to enforce this article by appropriate legislation. (Ratified January, 1964.)

Amendment XXV.

Procedures for Presidential Succession

Section 1. In case of the removal of the President from office or of his death or resignation, the Vice President shall become President.

Section 2. Whenever there is a vacancy in the office of the Vice President, the President shall nominate a Vice President who shall take office upon confirmation by a majority vote of both Houses of Congress.

Section 3. Whenever the President transmits to the President pro tempore of the Senate and the Speaker of the House of Representatives his written declaration that he is unable to discharge the powers and duties of his office, and until he transmits to them a written declaration to the contrary, such powers and duties shall be discharged by the Vice President as Acting President.

Section 4. Whenever the Vice President and a majority of either the principal officers of the executive departments or of such other body as Congress may by law provide, transmit to the President pro tempore of the Senate and the Speaker of the House of Representatives their written declaration that the President is unable to discharge the powers and duties of his office, the Vice President shall immediately assume the powers and duties of the office as Acting President.

Thereafter, when the President transmits to the President pro tempore of the Senate and the Speaker of the House of Representatives his written declaration that no inability exists, he shall resume the powers and duties of his office unless the Vice President and a majority of either the principal officers of the executive department or of such other body as Congress may by law provide, transmit within four days to the President pro tempore of the Senate and the Speaker of the House of Representatives their written declaration that the President is unable to discharge the powers and duties of his office. Thereupon Congress shall decide the issue, assembling within forty-eight hours for that purpose if not in session. If the Congress, within twenty-one days after receipt of the latter written declaration, or, if Congress is not in session, within twenty-one days after Congress is required to assemble, determines by two-thirds vote of both Houses that the President is unable to discharge the powers and duties of his office, the Vice President shall continue to discharge the same as Acting President; otherwise, the President shall resume the powers and duties of his office. (Ratified February, 1967.)

Amendment XXVI.

Voting Age Lowered to Eighteen

Section 1. The right of citizens of the United States, who are eighteen years of age or older, to vote shall not be denied or abridged by the United States or by any State on account of age.

Section 2. The Congress shall have power to enforce this article by appropriate legislation. (Ratified July, 1971.)

This is the original text and section numbers. Descriptive headings have been added by editors. Passages in brackets indicate that they were changed by Amendments.

Biographies of Important Framers

Dickinson, John (1732-1808)

Dickinson was born in Maryland. He was the son of a wealthy farm family. He was educated by private tutors and then studied law in Philadelphia and London. He set up his first law practice in Philadelphia, where he served in the Pennsylvania legislature. Dickinson became famous all over the colonies for opposing British taxation. He served in the Continental Army. He headed the committee that wrote the Articles of Confederation. By 1786, he believed the Articles needed to be changed. Dickinson was highly respected. He made important contributions to the Philadelphia Convention but left early because of illness. He spent his later years writing about politics.

Ellsworth, Oliver (1745-1807)

Ellsworth was a member of a rich Connecticut family. He graduated from the College of New Jersey. He taught school and served as a minister before going into law. He was soon considered one of Connecticut's best lawyers. Ellsworth served in the Continental Congress. He did not want the national government to become too strong. He also did not want the people to be given too much power. Ellsworth did not sign the Constitution, although he later became Chief Justice of the Supreme Court.

Franklin, Benjamin (1706-1790)

Franklin was the oldest delegate to the Philadelphia Convention. He was one of the best-known men in America. Born into a poor family, Franklin became an inventor, scientist, diplomat, and publisher. He served as an ambassador to England and France and as governor of Pennsylvania. At the convention, Franklin was a compromiser. He sometimes brought the delegates together by making them laugh. He played an important role in creating the Great Compromise. He favored a strong national government and argued that the Framers should trust the judgment of the people. Although he was in poor health in 1787, he missed few—if any—sessions. He was carried to and from the meeting place in a special chair. Although he did not agree with everything in the Constitution, he believed that no other convention could come up with a better document.

Gerry, Elbridge (1744-1814)

Gerry was born into a wealthy family in Massachusetts. He attended Harvard, learning politics from Samuel Adams, a revolutionary leader. Gerry protested against British policies and signed the Declaration of Independence. Gerry often changed his mind about political issues. For example, after Shays' Rebellion, he spoke against giving the common people too much power. But he still argued for yearly elections and against giving the Senate, which was not elected by the people, too much power. Gerry refused to sign the Constitution and worked against ratification. Throughout his life, he served in a variety of offices. He died in 1814 while serving as Vice President.

Hamilton, Alexander (1755-1804)

Alexander Hamilton was one of the brightest delegates at the Philadelphia Convention. He was born in the British West Indies. As a young man, he traveled to New York City, where he attended college until the American Revolution. He was very active in the war, serving as an aide to George Washington. Afterwards, he studied law and entered law practice. He served in the Continental Congress and was one of the leaders in calling for a constitutional convention. As a delegate, he played a rather small role because he had to miss many sessions. He wanted a much stronger national government than did most of the other delegates. Hamilton worked hard for ratification in New York. He served in Washington's government as Secretary of the Treasury. In 1804, Hamilton was killed in a duel with Aaron Burr.

Madison, James (1751-1836)

James Madison is often called the "Father of the Constitution." He was born to a wealthy family in Virginia. He was taught at home and in private schools. He graduated from the College of New Jersey. While debating whether to become a lawyer or minister, Madison became involved in the American Revolution. In 1780, Madison was chosen to serve in the Continental Congress, where he played an important role. He was one of the most influential people calling for a constitutional convention. He came to the Philadelphia Convention with a plan for the new government. Madison took extensive notes at the convention and spoke more than 150 times. He also worked hard on several committees. Madison was a key figure in the battle for ratification. Following the convention, he served as a member of the U.S. House of Representatives, helping to write the Bill of Rights and organize the executive department. Under Jefferson, Madison served as Secretary of State. He then followed Jefferson as President. In retirement, Madison continued to speak out on public issues.

Martin, Luther (1748-1826)

Luther Martin was born in New Jersey around 1748. After graduating from the College of New Jersey, he taught school and studied the law. He moved to Maryland, where he began practicing law. He served as state attorney general and in the Continental Congress. At the convention, he was against increasing the power of the federal government. Because he believed in the rights of the states and of the people, Martin wanted each state to have an equal vote in Congress. He also wanted a bill of rights. Although he owned six slaves, Martin opposed slavery and spoke out against it. Martin left the convention and did not sign the Constitution. He fought against ratification in Maryland. Martin served almost 30 years as Maryland state attorney general.

Mason, George (1725-1792)

George Mason was born into a wealthy Virginia family. He studied law and lived on a large plantation near George Washington's home. For most of his life, Mason stayed out of public office. He did serve in the Virginia legislature but quit in 1769. At the Philadelphia Convention, Mason spoke often. He argued against giving the President too much power and for a bill of rights. He also spoke against slavery, although at his death, he owned 300 slaves himself. Mason did not sign the Constitution and fought against ratification. He died shortly after the ratification of the Bill of Rights.

Morris, Gouverneur (1752-1816)

Morris was born in New York to a wealthy family. Early in life, he lost a leg in a carriage accident. He graduated from King's College in New York City and then studied law. Many of his family and friends were Loyalists, but Morris sided with the Patriots. He served in the state militia as well as in the New York legislature and the Continental Congress. When he was defeated for Congress in 1779, Morris moved to Philadelphia to practice law. At the Philadelphia Convention, Morris gave more speeches than anyone else. He favored a strong national government ruled by the upper classes. He served on many committees and was the primary writer of the actual document. After the convention, Morris spent ten years in Europe. He served briefly in the Senate, but then retired.

Pinckney, Charles (1757-1824)

Charles Pinckney was born in South Carolina, the son of a rich lawyer and planter. Pinckney trained as a lawyer. He served in the militia during the American Revolution, was captured by the British, and was a prisoner until 1781. He served in the Continental Congress and the South Carolina legislature. At the Philadelphia Convention, Pinckney spoke often. He was a good speaker who helped create the compromises that made the Constitution possible. After the convention, he held a variety of offices, including governor and U.S. senator. He worked to give the vote to all white males.

Randolph, Edmund (1753-1813)

Randolph was born into a well-known Virginia family of lawyers. He attended William and Mary College and then studied law under his father. The Revolution split the family. Edmund's father, mother, and two sisters were Loyalists while Edmund and his uncle were Patriots. Randolph served in the Continental Congress and as governor of Virginia. He gave the first major speech at the Philadelphia Convention, in which he criticized the Articles of Confederation. As leader of the Virginia delegation, he presented the Virginia Plan to the convention. Although the Constitution included many ideas similar to those in the Virginia Plan, he did not sign the document. However, George Washington persuaded Randolph to support ratification. Randolph served as Attorney General and Secretary of State under Washington.

Rutledge, John (1739-1800)

Rutledge was born in South Carolina and was taught at home — by his father and a tutor. He then studied law in London. He returned to South Carolina, where he practiced law and built a fortune. He was active in South Carolina politics in the 1760s and 1770s, serving in the Continental Congress and as governor. When the British seized Charleston, Rutledge had to flee to North Carolina. He gathered a force to recapture South Carolina. At the Philadelphia Convention, he was an important delegate, speaking often and well. He argued for the interests of the Southern states. Washington appointed Rutledge to the U.S. Supreme Court, where he served a brief time. He returned to South Carolina to serve on the state supreme court. In 1795, Washington again appointed him to the Supreme Court, this time as Chief Justice. The Senate rejected his nomination. He retired from public life after this defeat.

Sherman, Roger (1721-1793)

Born in 1721 in Massachusetts, Sherman spent most of his boyhood helping his father with farming and shoe-making chores. He read in whatever spare time he could find. In 1743, he moved to Connecticut, buying a store and entering politics. Sherman served in the state legislature and the Continental Congress, worked as a judge, and wrote essays and almanacs. He was one of the members of the committee that wrote the Declaration of Independence and the Articles of Confederation. Sherman attended nearly every session of the Philadelphia Convention and helped create the Great Compromise. He also worked hard to get Connecticut to ratify the Constitution. He later served in the House of Representatives and Senate.

Washington, George (1732-1798)

George Washington was born in Virginia. He grew up there on several plantations along the Potomac and Rapahannock Rivers. In 1753, he began his service to his country. It continued throughout his life, although he would rather have lived as a simple farmer. Washington's efforts as commander of the Continental Army are well known. After the Revolution, Washington returned to his home, Mount Vernon. At first he did not want to attend the Philadelphia Convention. His friends convinced him that he should. He was elected president of the convention, but spoke little. Nearly everyone thought that Washington would be the first President of the United States. He was, serving from 1788-1796. When he died, Washington's will said that his slaves should be freed when his wife Martha died.

Wilson, James (1741-1798)

Wilson was born and educated in Scotland. He arrived in America in 1765. He taught and studied law and set up a legal practice in Pennsylvania. He was active in the revolutionary effort, voting for independence and signing the Declaration. After the war, he defended Loyalists and their sympathizers. This action made many people in Pennsylvania angry. But by the 1780s, Wilson was again elected to the Continental Congress. Wilson was an important delegate to the Philadelphia Convention. He spoke even more often than Madison. Wilson led the ratification effort in Pennsylvania. He was appointed to the Supreme Court.

Yates, Robert (1738-1801)

Yates was born and educated in New York. He became a lawyer and set up practice in Albany. He served in several offices, spending the greatest amount of time as a justice of the New York Supreme Court (1777-1798). Yates left the Philadelphia Convention because he believed it had gone beyond its instructions from Congress. He worked against ratification. Yates kept notes of the parts of the convention he attended. These notes have been useful to historians.

Glossary

amendment. A change in or addition to a document.

American Revolution. The American colonies' war for independence from Great Britain. It took place from 1775 to 1781.

Articles. The major parts of the Constitution.

Articles of Confederation. The first constitution of the United States. It was adopted in 1781 and replaced in 1788 by our present Constitution.

basic rights. The rights to life, liberty, and property which everyone should have.

bill. A proposed law sent to the legislature for approval.

Bill of Rights. The first ten amendments to the Constitution. It contains the basic rights which the federal government may not interfere with.

board of inquiry. A group formed to study or investigate a situation.

Brown v. Board of Education. The 1954 Supreme Court case that decided that segregated schools were unconstitutional. The Court said that separate schools denied black children the equal protection of the laws.

cabinet. A group made up of the heads of the departments of the executive branch. They advise the President.

capital punishment. Death as a legal punishment for a crime; also called the death penalty.

checks and balances. The sharing and balancing of power among different branches of government so no one branch can completely control the others.

Chief Justice. The head of a court. The Chief Justice of the United States is head of the Supreme Court.

citizen. A person who is a member of a nation.

Civil War. The war between the Northern and Southern states that took place in our country between 1861-1865.

Civil War Amendments. The Thirteenth, Fourteenth, and Fifteenth Amendments to the Constitution passed after the Civil War. These amendments were intended to give the newly-freed slaves the rights of citizens.

civic virtue. Putting the common welfare above individual interests.

clause. A phrase in the Constitution.

colony. A settlement or territory ruled by another country.

common defense. Protection of the people from enemies.

common welfare. The good of the community as a whole.

compromise. A way to settle differences by each side agreeing to give up part of what it wants.

conflict. Disagreement; argument.

Congress. The national legislature of the United States. Congress has two houses, the Senate and the House of Representatives.

consent. To agree.

constitution. A set of rules and laws that tells how a government is organized and run.

constitutional government. A government in which the powers of the ruler or rulers are limited by a constitution. The rulers must obey the constitution.

Continental Congress. The national legislature which governed the American colonies from 1774 until the adoption of the Articles of Confederation.

convention. A formal assembly or meeting.

cross-examine. To question witnesses testifying for the other side in a trial.

Declaration of Independence. The statement which gave the reasons why the colonists wanted to free themselves from British rule. It was signed by the members of Congress on July 4, 1776.

delegate. A person picked to act for or represent others, usually at a convention or meeting.

democracy. A form of government in which power is held by the people. The people exercise their power either directly or through elected representatives.

dictator. A head of government who has unlimited power.

dictatorial government. A government in which the rulers have unlimited power.

discrimination. Unfair treatment of people because of their race, religion, or sex.

diversity. Having people of many different backgrounds.

domestic tranquility. As used in the Preamble, this phrase means a peaceful situation within our country.

due process. The right to be protected from unfair government procedures and laws.

enforce. To make people obey the law.

equal protection. Treating all individuals or groups of people equally under the law.

establishment clause. The part of the First Amendment that says the government cannot set up an official religion.

executive. The person who has power to carry out, or enforce, the law.

executive branch. The branch of government that carries out the laws made by the legislative branch.

federal system. A form of government in which power is divided between a central government and state and local governments.

Founders. The people who were important in the establishment of the United States.

Framers. The delegates to the Philadelphia Convention of 1787.

free exercise clause. The part of the First Amendment which says the government shall not deny a person the right to practice his religion.

freedom of expression. The freedoms of speech, press, assembly, and petition that are protected by the First Amendment.

freedom of religion. The right to hold whatever religious beliefs we wish without interference by the government.

fugitive slave clause. The part of the Constitution which said that slaves who escaped must be returned to their owners.

general welfare. The good of all the people.

government. The organization through which political authority is used.

grandfather clause. The law that allowed whites who could not pass a literacy test to vote if their grandfathers had been able to vote.

Great Compromise. The plan accepted at the Philadelphia Convention that called for Congress to have two houses. The Senate would have two senators from each state. In the House of Representatives, the number of representatives from each state would be based on its population.

hearing. A meeting in which citizens give their views to public officials.

House of Representatives. One house of Congress. The number of representatives from each state is based on its population.

immigrant. A person who leaves his or her native land to settle in another country.

impeach. To accuse a public official of committing a crime while he or she is in office.

indentured servant. A person who agreed to work for someone for a set period of time in return for the cost of coming to America.

interests. Those things which are to one's advantage or benefit.

interpret. To explain the meaning of something.

judicial branch. The branch of government that interprets and applies the laws and settles disputes.

judicial review. The power of the courts to say the Constitution does not allow the government to do something.

Judiciary Act of 1789. The law that established the federal court system below the Supreme Court.

justices. Members of the Supreme Court.

law. A bill that has been passed by the legislature and signed by the executive.

legislative branch. The branch of government that makes the laws.

liberty. Freedom.

limits. Restrictions; boundaries.

literacy tests. Tests given to people to prove they are able to read and write. These tests were used in the South to keep black people from voting.

Loyalists. Americans who supported Great Britain during the Revolution.

majority. More than half.

national government. The organization having political authority in a nation.

natural rights. The rights to life, liberty, and property.

Northwest Ordinance of 1787. An important law passed by Congress under the Articles of Confederation. The law provided for settling the western lands and organizing new states.

participation. Taking part in or sharing in the activities of a group or organization.

Patriots. Those Americans who supported the war for independence against Great Britain.

persecute. To cause suffering to a person or group because of their beliefs.

petition. A formal, written request.

Philadelphia Convention. The meeting held in Philadelphia in 1787 at which the U.S. Constitution was written.

plantation. A large farm usually found in the Southern states.

politics. The activities of getting and holding public office and making laws.

poll tax. A tax that voters in many states had to pay before they could vote.

population. The number of people living in an area.

Preamble. The introduction to the Constitution. In the Preamble, the Framers (1) stated that the people established the government, and (2) listed the purposes of the government.

procedures. The methods or steps taken to accomplish something.

property. Something that is owned.

ratify. Approve.

ratification. The formal approval of the Constitution by the states.

ratifying conventions. Meetings held in the states to approve the Constitution.

representatives. People elected to act for others.

republican government. A government in which power is held by the people who elect representatives to run the government for the common welfare.

responsibility. Duty or obligation.

retire. To leave a job upon reaching a certain age.

secretaries. The heads of the departments in the executive branch who act as advisers to the President.

segregation. The separation of people in schools and other public places because of their race.

self-sufficient. Able to provide most of one's own needs.

Senate. One house of Congress. Each state has two members in the Senate.

separation of powers. The division of powers among the different branches of government. In the United States, powers are divided among the legislative, executive, and judicial branches.

slavery. Ownership of human beings as property.

Supreme Court. The highest court in the United States.

testify. Give information or evidence, as at a hearing or trial.

three-fifths clause. The part of the Constitution that counted each slave as three-fifths of a person to determine how many representatives a state would have in Congress.

trade. The buying and selling of goods.

treaty. An official agreement between two or more governments or rulers.

unconstitutional. Not allowed by the Constitution; illegal.

veto. The power of the President to refuse to approve a bill passed by Congress.

witness. A person who is called to give evidence before a court.

Suggested Reading for Students

Avi. *Night Journeys*. New York: Pantheon Books, 1979.

Burningham, John. *Mr. Gumppy's Outing*. New York: H. Holt & Co., 1971.

Commanger, Henry Steele. *The Great Constitution: A Book for Young Americans*. New York: Bobbs-Merrill, 1961.

Faber, Harold and Doris Faber. *We the People: The Story of the Constitution Since 1787*. New York: Schribner, 1987.

Fritz, Jean. *Shh! We're Writing the Constitution*. New York: Putnam, 1987.

Fritz, Jean. *Will You Sign Here, John Hancock?* New York: Putnam, 1976.

Fritz, Jean. *Why Don't You Get a Horse, Sam Adams?* New York: Putnam, 1974.

Hilton, Suzanne. *We the People: The Way We Were, 1783-1793*. Philadelphia: Westminster Press, 1981.

Levy, Elizabeth. *If You Were There When They Signed the Constitution*. New York: Scholastic Inc., 1987.

McPhillipps, Martin. *The Constitutional Convention*. Morristown: Silver, Burdett & Ginn, Inc., 1985.

Maestro, Betsy. *A More Perfect Union: The Story of Our Constitution*. Boston: Lothrop, Lee & Shepard Books, 1987.

Morris, Richard. *The Constitution*. New York: Lerner, 1985.

O'Dell, Scott. *Zia*. Boston: Houghton Mifflin & Co., 1976.

Peterson, Helen. *The Making of the U.S. Constitution*. New York: Garrard, 1974.

Prolman, Marilyn. *The Story of the Constitution*. Chicago: Children's Press, 1969.

Seuss, Dr. *Yertle the Turtle*. New York: Random House, 1974.

Spier, Peter. *We the People: The Story of the U. S. Constitution*. New York: Doubleday & Co., 1987.

Taylor, Mildred. *Song of the Trees*. New York: Bantam Books, 1984.

Turner, Ann. *Nettie's Trip South*. New York: Macmillan Publishing Company, 1987.

Uchida, Yoshiko. *Journey to Topaz*. New York: Charles Schribner's Sons, 1971.

Winn, Marie. *Shiver, Gobble and Snore*. New York: Simon and Schuster, 1971.

Suggested Reading for Teachers

Bernstein, Richard B. *Are We To Be A Nation? The Making of the Constitution.* Cambridge: Harvard University Press, 1987.

Bowen, Catherine Drinker. *Miracle at Philadelphia.* Boston: Little, Brown & Co., 1986.

Collier, James L. and Christopher Collier. *Decision in Philadelphia.* New York: Random House, 1985.

Farrand, Max. *The Framing of the Constitution of the United States.* 1913. Reprint. New Haven: Yale University Press, 1987.

Hamilton, Alexander, James Madison, and John Jay. *The Federalist Papers,* ed. by Clinton Rossiter. New York: Mentor Books, New American Library, 1961.

Hand, Learned. *The Bill of Rights.* Cambridge: Harvard University Press, 1958.

Johnston, Johanna. *They Led the Way: Fourteen American Women.* New York: Scholastic, 1973.

Kamen, Michael, ed. *The Origins of the American Constitution: A Documentary History.* New York: Penguin Books, 1986.

Kelly, Alfred H. and Winfred A. Harbison. *The American Constitution: Its Origins and Development.* New York: W.W. Norton, 1983.

Kerber, Linda. *Women of the Republic: Intellect & Ideology in Revolutionary America.* New York: W.W. Norton, 1986.

Morris, Richard. *Witnesses at the Creation: Hamilton, Madison, Jay, and the Constitution.* New York: Holt, Rinehart & Winston, 1985.

Murphy, Paul L. *The Constitution in the Twentieth Century.* Washington, D.C.: American Historical Association, 1986.

Rodell, Fred. *55 Men: The Story of the Constitution.* New York: Macmillan Publishing Company, 1966.